W9-CLB-547

a batch of QuiltSoup

Fun
Patchwork
and Easy
Appliqué
Patterns

Barbara J. Jones

Martingale®
Create with Confidence

Dedication

To all of you who have contributed to QuiltSoup's success throughout the years—from my family, friends, and helpers to all of our customers. Thank you for your support. It has allowed me to do what I love with the hope of making a living at it!

A Special Acknowledgment

A very special thanks goes to Catherine Timmons, owner of Cat's Attic Quilting in Bountiful, Utah, for expert machine quilting. Her work always enhances mine. I also thank Jan Child for help with the piecing and each lovely binding on every quilt we now make. I hate to bind, but Jan doesn't mind it. A bonus for me is that her bindings always put mine to shame! I owe a huge debt of gratitude to these ladies. They work tirelessly and never complain when they lose sleep to meet my unreasonable deadlines.

A Batch of QuiltSoup:
Fun Patchwork and Easy Appliqué Patterns
© 2012 by Barbara J. Jones

Martingale®
19021 120th Ave. NE, Ste. 102
Bothell, WA 98011-9511 USA
ShopMartingale.com

Printed in China
17 16 15 14 13 12   8 7 6 5 4 3 2 1

Library of Congress Cataloging-in-Publication Data is available upon request.

ISBN: 978-1-60468-157-4

Mission Statement

Dedicated to providing quality products and service to inspire creativity.

Credits

President & CEO: Tom Wierzbicki
Editor in Chief: Mary V. Green
Design Director: Paula Schlosser
Managing Editor: Karen Costello Soltys
Technical Editor: Rebecca Kemp Brent
Copy Editor: Sheila Chapman Ryan
Production Manager: Regina Girard
Illustrators: Robin Strobel and Missy Shepler
Cover & Text Designer: Regina Girard
Photographer: Brent Kane

No part of this product may be reproduced in any form, unless otherwise stated, in which case reproduction is limited to the use of the purchaser. The written instructions, photographs, designs, projects, and patterns are intended for the personal, noncommercial use of the retail purchaser and are under federal copyright laws; they are not to be reproduced by any electronic, mechanical, or other means, including informational storage or retrieval systems, for commercial use. Permission is granted to photocopy patterns for the personal use of the retail purchaser. Attention teachers: Martingale encourages you to use this book for teaching, subject to the restrictions stated above.

The information in this book is presented in good faith, but no warranty is given nor results guaranteed. Since Martingale has no control over choice of materials or procedures, the company assumes no responsibility for the use of this information.

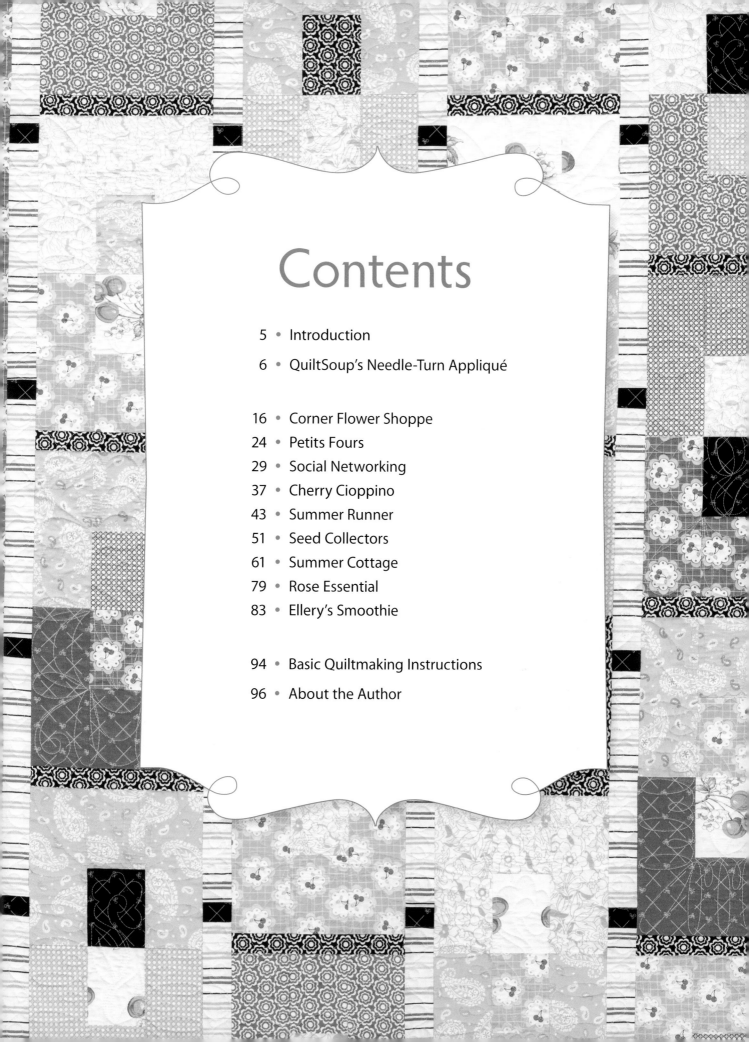

Contents

Introduction

A Batch of QuiltSoup is a collection of charming and whimsical quilts from the company by the same name. QuiltSoup specializes in needle-turn appliqué quilt patterns designed for confident beginners through advanced quiltmakers. Don't let the word *appliqué* scare you—these patterns are easy to finish in this lifetime!

The section called "QuiltSoup's Needle-Turn Appliqué" (page 6) is a complete class on QuiltSoup's preferred methods, from my favorite supplies and tools to making a quilter's knot and executing nearly invisible appliqué stitches.

Next are the projects, loosely organized by level of difficulty, with easiest first. You'll find step-by-step instructions, appliqué pattern pieces, and recipes with some of the projects. The recipes range from soup to dessert and represent some of my favorites.

"Basic Quiltmaking Instructions" (page 94) outlines layering and basting a quilt top and binding the edges of a quilt with a double-fold bias binding—which is the only kind I use.

Lastly, you'll find information about QuiltSoup. I hope you enjoy making the quilts as much as I do.

~Barbara

QuiltSoup's Needle-Turn Appliqué

My quilts can be made using any method of appliqué you prefer. If you aren't a fan of handwork or if you're in a hurry, fusible appliqué may be the way to go for you. You can stitch the appliqués by machine, if that's your real love. I prefer needle-turn appliqué, so the information in this section is about learning to do needle-turn appliqué. If you're not sold on that method, have a look at the reasons why I love it below. Then, if you want to give it a try, you'll find all you need to know about it in this section.

I prefer needle-turn appliqué for a variety of reasons. First, I love quilting for the journey, not just the destination. I find the repetition of handwork to be calming. In our busy lives, it affords a respite from a hectic pace. I usually stitch for several hours every evening, and I can always tell when I've missed a few days—I get grumpy!

Second, I find appliqué interesting enough to keep me engaged without being so challenging that I have to concentrate too hard. I can stitch in a comfortable place (on the couch) and watch (mostly listen to) a movie, visit with friends, or tune out a conversation that I'm not interested in. (You know you do this too!)

Lastly, I love the portability of a needle-turn project in process. I always have a block of one kind or another prepared so I can just grab my supplies and go. I find that time evaporates when I'm stitching and appliqué makes waiting or long road trips tolerable. I can stitch at a ball game, at the doctor's office, on a plane, or in the airport. I'm not hunched over a sewing machine that's tied to a specific room in the house. To me, hand appliqué is like having Wi-Fi, while sewing at my machine is like being tethered to dial-up Internet access.

As with all techniques, you need a few tools and a method to do the job. In general, these are the steps I follow and the tools I use for needle-turn appliqué.

Basic Appliqué Tool Kit

For needle-turn appliqué, as for any craft, the right tools are important to make the process go smoothly. Assemble your basic appliqué tool kit and have it ready for stitching at home or on the go.

Having the right tools makes needle-turn appliqué a breeze!

Needles

I use John James size 11 milliner's needles for needle-turn appliqué. These needles have long shafts that are useful for turning under the seam allowances while working my way around a patch. They're very fine and bend easily, so keep a supply at hand. The needle eyes are very tiny, so a needle threader (I like Clover's Desk Needle Threader) often comes in handy.

Thread

The goal is to achieve an invisible stitch, and a fine thread will help do that. Choose a 50-weight cotton thread, which is fine enough to sink into the fibers of a patch but strong enough that it won't break.

Use 100% cotton thread that matches the color of each appliqué patch. My favorite appliqué thread is Aurifil 50-weight cotton thread; MasterPiece 100% cotton by Superior Threads is another excellent choice.

A Kit of Many Colors

MasterPiece thread is available in a product called a Frosted Donut, a plastic bobbin-keeper ring containing prewound bobbins of 36 different colors, 85 yards of each color. The Donut (shown opposite) measures about 6" in diameter by 1" high, making it a dream for portability. Put a pack of needles, a travel-sized bottle of glue, appliqué scissors, and a charcoal marker inside a bag with the Donut for an appliqué kit that's small, lightweight, and easy to carry with you.

Thread Conditioners

Thread conditioners are applied to reduce thread tangling during hand appliqué. Their effects can vary, and using a thread conditioner is not essential. Two common forms are beeswax and a silicon-based product called Thread Heaven. Although it does decrease tangling, beeswax changes the feel of the thread and makes it more visible. Thread Heaven doesn't change the appearance or texture of the thread, but it seems less efficient at preventing tangles. After experimenting with different types, I don't use thread conditioners; I prefer to work with thread straight from the spool.

Scissors

A good pair of appliqué scissors makes all the difference in the world and will definitely contribute to your success with appliqué. Select embroidery or weaver's scissors with blades that are 1½" to 2" long. Well-made scissors are usually expensive, but you get what you pay for. Choose a pair of scissors with fine points and tips that are extremely sharp. The sharp points can easily break if the scissors are dropped on a hard surface, so it's wise to purchase a protective leather sheath for storage when the scissors aren't use. Some quality scissor brands are Kai, Gingher, Omnigrid, and Dovo. When making your purchase, consider both initial sharpness and the ease of having the scissors resharpened.

Scissor Tips

I prefer Dovo's scissors for their fine points. However, it may be difficult to find someone who can do a good job of sharpening them, and this brand isn't as easy to find as some others.

Preparing Appliqué Templates

Pattern shapes are traced onto template material. The shapes are then cut out exactly on the traced line with paper scissors. Do *not* add a seam allowance to the templates.

I use two different kinds of template material: freezer paper and template plastic. Each has advantages and disadvantages.

Freezer Paper

Freezer paper is usually found in the canning section of the grocery store. The dull side is made of paper and not coated; I think of this as the "right side" of the freezer paper. This is the side that I trace and label on and the side that's facing up when I lay it over a pattern or on the fabric.

Freezer paper is lightweight enough to see through, so tracing patterns is easy. The weight of the paper also makes it easy to cut complex shapes. The back, or wrong side, of the freezer paper is shiny and has a coating that adheres the paper to other materials (or itself) when pressed with a hot iron. You can reuse paper templates until they no longer adhere. The paper also helps to stabilize a fabric shape when you're cutting or positioning it onto a block; think of a curvy tendril or vine. Freezer paper is less expensive than template plastic as well.

Because it's continuous for many yards, freezer paper can be used for large or long shapes. I use it for drawing and cutting vines, tendrils, long pumpkins, single-occurrence patches, and for all of my wool appliqués.

Template Plastic

Template plastic is readily available in most quilt shops. It's usually lightly frosted on one side and subtly textured on the reverse side. I think of the frosted side as the "right side," and trace or label patterns on the frosted side with a Sharpie fine-point permanent marker. I use template plastic for shapes that are repeated many times, such as leaves. I find that the plastic keeps its shape better than freezer paper; the edges don't wear down. I also use plastic for templates that need to be reversed, because it's quicker and easier for me to flip a template over than to prepare a second, reversed template from freezer paper.

Marking Appliqué Patches

Position each template on the fabric right side and trace its shape onto the fabric the number of times it appears in the design. (See "A Bit About Markers," opposite.) The marked line serves as the stitching line and provides a guide for cutting.

Where and how you position the template does matter. Bias grain has the most flexibility or "give" of any part of the fabric, especially the true bias, which is found at a 45° angle to the selvage. Bias edges work best for turning under seam allowances, so take advantage of that by placing the longest dimension of a template on the bias grain of the fabric. Think of a long, narrow leaf; place it on the fabric as shown, and then mark directly around it.

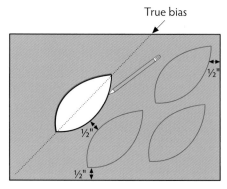

Place template with its longest dimension on the true bias and leave at least ½" between patches.

The only time I deviate from the bias placement is when I want to take advantage of a particular motif in the fabric, a technique called fussy cutting. Remember to leave at least ½" between patches for seam allowances, whether the shapes are fussy cut or not.

If you're using freezer-paper templates, iron them to the right side of the fabric with the iron on its wool setting. Trace around the template and remove the paper unless it's a very large or very curvy template. In those instances, trace around the template but leave the freezer paper in place until you've positioned the patch on the block to prevent fabric distortion.

A Bit About Markers

To mark on light-colored fabrics, use a .05 mm mechanical pencil. When using a standard pencil to mark numerous shapes, the pencil point broadens as it wears down, leading to inconsistent marks. This doesn't happen with a mechanical pencil, which always makes marks of a consistent width.

To mark on dark fabrics, I use a white charcoal pencil made by General's. These can usually be found in an art-supply store. I find that a line made with a chalk marker will wear away before I have finished all the stitching. Conversely, I definitely do not use markers with waxes or additives in them. These tend to make a line that's sharp, but I've had trouble with the marks never wearing away; also, wax markers can melt into the fabric when heat is applied. This means pressing makes the marks permanent, which is acceptable only if you're 100% perfect when you turn and stitch the seam allowances. For the rest of us, it's best to avoid permanent markers.

Charcoal pencils seem to lie between the two extremes. Their disadvantage is that they're soft and wear down quickly, broadening the drawn line; therefore, they must be sharpened frequently. It takes practice to sharpen them without breaking the charcoal point, but I've tried just about every marker on the market and the charcoal pencil suits me the best. That said, some of my friends prefer Bohin mechanical pencils with white lead. Try a few different marking tools to find your personal favorite.

Cutting Appliqué Patches

Before cutting the appliqué patches as traced, seam allowances must be added. There are two methods for determining how much seam allowance to add; try both to see which works better for you.

- Add a scant ¼" seam allowance outside the patch outline as you cut, estimating the seam allowance by eye. While this seam allowance is too large for appliqué and will need to be trimmed as the appliqué is stitched, the extra width allows you to cut away any raveling and stitch only clean edges. Large or complex pieces are particularly susceptible to fraying as they're handled, which can lead to less than stellar results in your appliqué.
- Cut the seam allowances by eye to ⅛", an appliqué-ready width. This eliminates the redundancy of trimming the seam allowances a second time.

Cutting Background Fabric

When patches are appliquéd to a background piece of fabric, some "take up" tends to occur. If you begin with background fabric that measures 15½" square, it may measure only 15⅛" to 15¼" when the appliqué is finished. For this reason, my instructions are for cutting over-sized backgrounds (1" larger than necessary) that will be trimmed to size when the appliqué and pressing are complete. For example, a block intended to finish 15½" square, including seam allowances, will initially be cut 16½" square.

Don't Be Without

One notion that I find invaluable for trimming backgrounds is an Omnigrid 20½" square ruler. I put off buying one for a number of years because I thought they were pricey and that I could do the job with the rulers I had. Both are true, but I'm sorry I waited as long as I did to buy one; this large square ruler makes the job easier and more accurate. Add one to your Christmas or birthday wish list.

Positioning Appliqués

My appliqué patterns are not so complicated that exact patch placement is necessary. I use three methods, singly or in combination, to position patches.

- The method I use 95% of the time is to judge the position by eye, without measuring. I don't think it's crucial whether a leaf is ⅛" or ¼" from the bottom of a stem, for example. Simply arrange the parts of the design until you're happy with how they look. Sometimes I find I want to add or subtract a leaf on a particular stem and I do so. I suggest you place the patches so they look good to you—even if they vary a bit from the placement shown in the book.

- To align patches that overlap one another, make hash marks in the seam allowances at the spots where the patches intersect. Mark the overlapping areas on the original templates and transfer the markings to the seam allowances as each patch is traced onto the fabric.

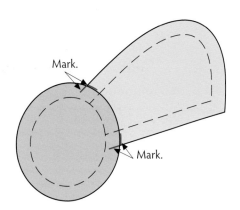

Make hash marks in the seam allowances of overlapping appliqués where they meet.

- When positioning patches that absolutely must fit together perfectly, place pins straight up and down through the top patch first, and then through the bottom patch at three key points on every set of patches. Key points are unique identifiers on the patches, such as leaf tips. Secure the pins and glue the patches together. If the match is particularly difficult or tricky,

baste the two pieces together about ¼" inside the stitching line all the way around the patches.

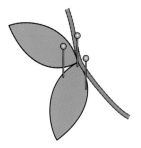

When matching is critical, hold the appliqué in place with three vertical pins until it can be basted or glued.

Holding Patches in Place

Once the appliqués are positioned, they must be held in place temporarily until they're securely stitched. I often use a combination of glue and hand basting to hold my patches for stitching; pins are another option.

For hand basting, use white, 100% cotton thread to avoid dyes and tiny fibers that could discolor the appliqué patches. Run a basting stitch all the way around the appliqué, about ¼" *inside* the stitching line.

For glue basting, I use Roxanne's Glue-Baste-It or Jillily Studio's Appli-Glue. When glue basting, less is more; both of these products have very small dispenser tips for applying tiny dots of glue. Work in a grid, placing tiny drops of glue about 1" apart on the wrong side of the appliqué patch. Fold back about half of the patch to apply glue while holding the other half in place with your other hand. Gluing in a close grid prevents distortions in the background fabric. Keep all of the basting glue ½" inside the stitching line, not on the seam allowances.

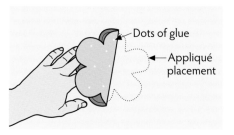

Turn back half of the shape at a time for gluing.

Appliqués can also be basted with ½"-long appliqué pins. The greatest drawback to pin basting is the possibility that the appliqué thread will become tangled around the pins. Pinning from the wrong side of the background fabric can reduce the chance of tangling.

Pin Tip

Pin basting seems unnecessarily complex to me and isn't my preferred method, but others use nothing else. To reduce complications, baste and stitch one appliqué at a time to avoid most overlapping prior to final stitching. Use short appliqué pins, which are engineered to minimize tangling.

Preparing to Stitch

Before you can begin stitching, you need to do three more things: thread your needle, make a quilter's knot in your thread, and find a comfortable place to sit for appliquéing!

Thread the Needle

Use a single length of thread, 12" to 15" long. Longer lengths are more likely to tangle or fray while you're stitching. This length is about the distance from the tip of your middle finger to your elbow, so it's easy to measure without a ruler. Stitch with a single (not doubled) strand of thread.

Ending Tangles

When the thread tail begins to fray or wear, it may tangle and knot around the working portion of the thread. Keep an eye on the tail end and snip it off when it begins to fray.

Knot a Problem

Knots in the appliqué thread can be frustrating, especially when one forms near the end of the stitches needed for a patch. When a knot in the working thread proves impossible to undo, clip just beyond the knot and tuck the thread end underneath the patch. Tie a new knot in the working thread and begin stitching about three stitches before the break, overlapping and reinforcing a few stitches. Use the same holes for the new stitches so that they're invisible.

Make a Quilter's Knot

With a little practice, it's easy to make a clean, small knot at the end of the thread to secure the first stitches without being obvious. These instructions are geared toward right-handed stitchers; reverse them if you're left-handed.

1. Lay the end of the thread farthest from the needle horizontally over the tip of your right index finger. Place the needle on top of the thread to hold the thread end against your index finger.

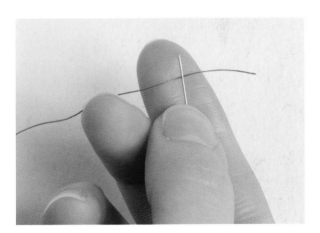

2. With your left hand, wrap the thread around the needle twice as if making a French knot.

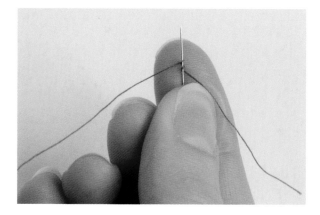

3. Pinch the wrapped thread around the needle securely with the right thumb and index finger.

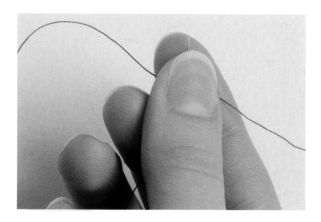

4. Pull the needle through the wraps with the left hand. Slide the wraps down the thread to its end, tightening them as you go, to create a small clean knot.
5. Trim the thread tail below the knot if necessary.

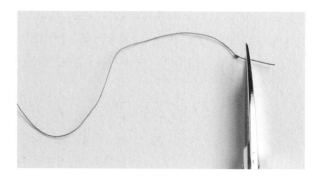

Get Comfortable

A comfortable chair and position—a stress-free way to sit—are important to your stitching pleasure and success. Some stitchers prefer to rest their arms on a stable surface like a tabletop while they stitch, and many benefit from raising their work up to a comfortable stitching distance. If you don't sit at a table, try using a small pillow resting in your lap to raise the work and support your lower arms.

If it's comfortable, sit with your legs crossed. Every time you rethread your needle, uncross your legs and recross them with the other one on top. A little movement releases stress and may help avoid blood-clot formation during long, stationary appliqué sessions.

It's really important to have good lighting when appliquéing. OttLites and numerous other small task lights are available to shine light directly onto your work. If you wear glasses (reading glasses or otherwise) but have trouble focusing on your stitches, confirm your prescription and invest in a new pair if needed.

Turn Up the Light
Hotel rooms are notorious for their poor lighting. For better working light, remove the lampshade while you stitch.

The Appliqué Stitch

To achieve an almost invisible stitch, use a small ladder stitch for needle-turn appliqué. The ladder stitch leaves hardly any thread on the work's right side. Stitch with the right side of the work facing you and the appliqué-patch edge running horizontally rather than vertically for the easiest progress.

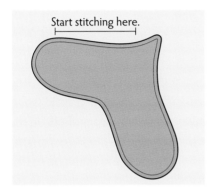

Orient the work as shown while stitching.

1. Bring the needle to the right side through the background and appliqué fabrics two threads' width inside the stitching line and pull the thread through.

Starting Point

It's easier to begin stitching on an appliqué edge that's straight or has a gentle outside curve. Avoid starting in a tricky area whenever possible; it can be done, but why struggle?

2. Trim the seam allowances to about ⅛" as you work. Seam allowances narrower than ⅛" may fray, while wider allowances are too bulky. Using the needle tip, tuck the seam allowances under the patch along the stitching line, turning under about ¾" ahead of the preceding stitch at a time. Hold the turned seam allowances in place with your left thumb.

3. Insert the needle into the background fabric directly across from the spot where it emerged from the patch. To determine the location, lay the thread across the work at a 90° angle to the appliqué edge; insert the needle into the background fabric just as the thread crosses the appliqué's edge. The stitch length will be very short—just spanning the appliqué edge.

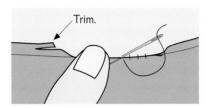

Trim seam allowance to ⅛" as it is turned under. Stitch length is exaggerated in this diagram.

4. Bring the needle back through the appliqué patch just inside the marked line and about ⅛" from the last stitch. Pull the thread lightly to make it snug against the fabric without gathering the work. Repeat the stitch from right to left around the patch; left-handed stitchers will work from left to right.

Unit Appliqué

Unit appliqué means stitching one appliqué to another before the unit, now treated as a single appliqué, is attached to the background.

The Tricky Stuff

Straight lines and outside curves can be stitched by following the steps above for the appliqué stitch. Other shapes may require special treatment, such as trimming or clipping, prior to stitching.

Inside curves. When the distance on the stitching line is greater than the distance on the cut edge of the patch, it's called an inside curve. The seam allowances must spread when turned under to lie flat beneath the patch. After trimming the seam allowance to ⅛", clip it perpendicular to the edge every ⅛" to ¼", spacing the clips evenly. Clip just to the marked stitching line, leaving just two threads intact. Use the side of the needle to swoop the seam allowances under in one motion (if you can) or in ¾" sections and stitch as usual.

Keep It Smooth

Fussing with a clipped edge leads to fraying. Avoid this by tucking the seam allowances under with as few motions as possible.

Leaf points. There are two methods for stitching sharp leaf points; I recommend you try both to see which works best for you. For either one, trim the seam allowances across the tip to the width you prefer for the rest of the appliqué shape, about ⅛". Once the left-hand side is turned under, hold the seam allowance in place with your thumb and pull the appliqué thread snug to create a sharp point before taking the next stitch.

Method 1. Turn under the seam allowances on the right-hand side of the leaf and stitch to the point. Bring the needle up just inside the stitching line at the exact point of the leaf.

Trim the seam
allowance at the tip.

Bring
needle
up here.

Turn under and stitch
the right-hand side.

Turn the seam allowances of the left-hand side of the leaf under, trimming again if necessary. Adjust the seam allowances to lie as flat as possible and continue stitching as usual. Lumps and bumps at the point mean there's too much bulk or the seam allowances aren't lying flat under the patch; if this happens, work the needle tip between the background and patch to smooth out the lumps.

Turn the left-hand side
under and finish stitching.

Method 2. Turn the right-hand seam allowance under and stitch to about ¾" from the point. Fold the blunted seam allowance under at the point, hold it in place with your left thumb, and continue stitching to the point. Bring the needle up just inside the stitching line at the point. Tuck the left-hand seam allowance under and continue stitching. This method distributes the bulk evenly on both sides of the point so that the patch lies flat.

Fold tip under first.

Really sharp points. For the sharpest, narrowest points, run a basting stitch through the center of the patch to hold it in place while stitching the right edge with one of the methods above. The basting will keep the point in place when neither seam allowance has been turned under, avoiding a droopy appearance. Once one side has been stitched in place, remove the basting; the point won't bend in either direction as it's sewn to the background.

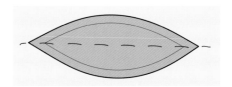

Baste the centerline of patches
with very narrow points.

Deep inner points. V-shaped points are very sharp inverted points; in my workshops, I call them "cleavage." They can be challenging to work. There are two ways to work a V point. Both begin by clipping the seam allowances at the V to within two threads of the marked stitching line.

Method 1. Fold under the fabric to the left of the clip in a straight line, temporarily tucking it beneath the appliqué patch. If basting glue interferes, gently pull the layers apart, or plan ahead and don't glue this section.

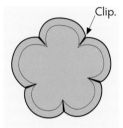 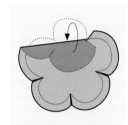

Tuck top portion underneath, beginning at the clip.

Stitch around the first part of the shape to the base of the clip. Pull the folded fabric back into its flat position, revealing its stitching line. Take a reinforcing stitch at the base of the clip, and then continue stitching around the shape. This method works well unless previous stitches interfere with folding the patch out of the way.

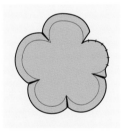

Stitch to the clip, then return the folded appliqué to its original position and continue stitching.

Method 2. Turn under the seam allowance to the left of the clip along the stitching line and place a single pin to hold it in place. Stitch around the first portion of the shape to the base of the clip. Make a single reinforcement stitch at the base of the clip, sew along the stitching line to the pin, and remove the pin.

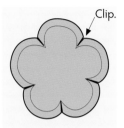

Turn under the seam allowance to the left of the clip and place a single pin.

Stitch to the clip, then stitch to the pin.

Corner Flower Shoppe

Pieced by Barbara Jones; quilted by Catherine Timmons

Finished quilt: 61" x 61"

FINISHED BLOCKS:

Flower blocks: 9" x 9" • Flowerpot blocks: 9" x 6"

Stem blocks: 9" x 6" • Awning blocks (for borders): 5" x 9"

I adore the flowers and pots in this quick-and-easy pieced quilt! The flower centers and leaves are the only appliqués on the quilt. Both are big, simple shapes, making this quilt a good place to start if you're new to appliqué.

Materials

Yardage is based on 42"-wide fabric.

1⅓ yards of white polka-dot fabric for alternate blocks

⅝ yard of white solid for block backgrounds

⅔ yard of lime-green striped fabric for borders and stems

½ yard of lime-green polka-dot fabric for borders, leaves, and flower centers

½ yard of raspberry print for flowers and flowerpots

⅜ yard of green large polka-dot fabric for flower centers and border corners

⅓ yard *each* of pink polka-dot, yellow polka-dot, and yellow daisy prints for flowers

⅓ yard of purple tiny ticking for flowers and flower centers

⅓ yard of orange print for flowers and flowerpot bands

⅛ yard of lime-green daisy print for leaves

⅛ yard of turquoise print for flower centers

3¾ yards of fabric for backing

½ yard of fabric for binding

65" x 65" piece of batting

Template plastic

Basic appliqué tool kit (see page 6)

Cutting

Patterns are on pages 22 and 23. Cutting for all patchwork pieces includes ¼" seam allowances.

From the white polka-dot fabric, cut:

2 strips, 12½" x 42"; crosscut into 8 rectangles, 9½" x 12½"

3 strips, 3½" x 42"; crosscut into 4 rectangles, 3½" x 9½", and 4 rectangles, 3½" x 12½"

3 strips, 2½" x 42"; crosscut into 40 squares, 2½" x 2½"

From the white solid, cut:

2 strips, 6½" x 42"; crosscut one strip into 8 rectangles, 4⅜" x 6½". Cut the remaining strip into 4 *each* using patterns A and A reversed (8 total).

3 strips, 2" x 42"; crosscut into 52 squares, 2" x 2"

From the lime-green striped fabric, cut:

2 strips, 9½" x 42"; crosscut into 12 rectangles, 5½" x 9½"

1 strip, 1¾" x 42"; crosscut into 4 rectangles, 1¾" x 6½"

From the lime-green polka-dot fabric, cut:

2 strips, 5½" x 42"; crosscut into 8 rectangles, 5½" x 9½"

4 using leaf pattern

2 using flower-center pattern

From the raspberry print, cut:

3 strips, 5" x 42"; crosscut *2 of the strips* into 12 squares, 5" x 5". Leave the remaining strip intact for flowerpots.

From the green large polka-dot fabric, cut:

2 strips, 5½" x 42"; crosscut into 4 rectangles, 5½" x 8½", and 4 rectangles, 3½" x 5½"

4 using flower-center pattern

From *each* of the pink polka-dot, yellow polka-dot, and yellow daisy prints, cut:

1 strip, 5" x 42"; crosscut into 8 squares, 5" x 5" (24 total)

From the purple tiny ticking, cut:

1 strip, 5" x 42"; crosscut into 8 squares, 5" x 5"

3 using flower-center pattern

From the orange print, cut:

1 strip, 5" x 42"; crosscut into 8 squares, 5" x 5"

1 strip, 2" x 42"

From the lime-green daisy print, cut:

4 using leaf pattern reversed

From the turquoise print, cut:

4 using flower-center pattern

Beautiful Background
I used a Kona fabric called Snow for the white background solid.

Make the Blocks

Piece the individual blocks to create backgrounds for the appliqués and complete the quilt.

Flower Blocks

1. On the wrong side, lightly mark each 2" white square diagonally from corner to corner with a pencil.
2. Place a marked square on the upper-left corner of a raspberry-print 5" square, right sides together and raw edges matched. Sew along the diagonal line, about one thread width to the outside of the marked line; this allows for fabric taken up when the seam is pressed.

3. Fold the small square toward the corner as shown and press. Fold the square back down into the sewing position and trim both fabrics ¼" beyond the seam line. Return the corner triangle to its position and press again. Make 12 total from raspberry print and eight *each* of pink polka dot, yellow polka dot, yellow daisy print, purple tiny ticking, and orange print.

Make 52.

Pressing Tip
Pressing the unit before trimming reduces stretch along the bias seam and yields a more accurate unit.

4. Orienting the white corners as shown, join four matching squares into a four-patch unit. Make three raspberry-print Flower blocks and two *each* of pink polka dot, yellow polka dot, yellow daisy print, purple tiny ticking, and orange print.

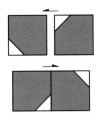

5. Prepare the 13 flower centers for needle-turn appliqué and stitch one at the center of each Flower block. Use the photograph on page 16 as a color guide.
6. Press the completed blocks. Working from the wrong side, cut away the fabric behind the flower center to reduce bulk, leaving a ¼" seam allowance.

Flowerpot Blocks

1. Sew the orange 2"-wide strip and raspberry 5"-wide strip together along one long edge. Press the seam allowances toward the raspberry fabric. Mark and cut four complete pots from this strip set using pattern B (page 23). Position the orange strip at the wide end of each flowerpot.
2. Sew a white A piece to the left side of a flowerpot and a white A reversed piece to the right side. Press the seam allowances toward the triangles. The Flowerpot blocks measure 6½" x 9½"; make four.

Make 4.

Stem Blocks

1. Sew a white 4⅜" x 6½" rectangle to each long side of a striped 1¾" x 6½" rectangle. Press the seam allowances toward the stem. Make four.

2. Position a daisy-print leaf on the left side of each stem and a lime-green leaf on the right side as shown. Be certain the finished edges of the leaves are at least ½" inside the block's raw edges. Glue baste, and then appliqué the leaves to the block; press. Make four.

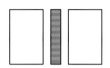

Make 4.

Awning Blocks

1. Draw a line on the wrong side of each white polka-dot 2½" square, marking diagonally from corner to corner. Place a square over one corner of each lime-green striped and polka-dot 5½" x 9½" rectangle.

2. Sew each seam just outside the marked lines, following the instructions for the Flower blocks. Press the seams toward the corner triangles on the striped blocks and away from the triangles on the dotted blocks to create opposing seam allowances as an aid to matching the seams later. Trim the seam allowances and finish as for the Flower blocks.

3. Repeat to sew the remaining squares to the opposite ends of the Awning blocks. Make 12 striped and eight dotted blocks.

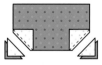

Make 8 dotted.

Make 12 striped.

Assemble the Quilt Top

Once the blocks are complete, the quilt-top assembly begins. It's a simple nine-patch structure with borders that's easy to complete.

Corner Sections

1. Sew a white polka-dot 3½" x 9½" rectangle to the top of a raspberry Flower block. Press the seam allowances toward the white rectangle. Make three raspberry and one pink.

2. Sew a white polka-dot 3½" x 12½" rectangle to the *left* side of a step 1 unit; press the seam allowances toward the rectangle. Make two. Sew a white polka-dot 3½" x 12½" rectangle to the *right* side of a remaining step 1 unit; press the seam allowances toward the rectangle. Make two.

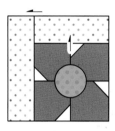 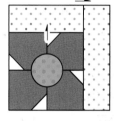

Make 2.   Make 2
(1 raspberry and 1 pink).

3. Stitch a white polka-dot 9½" x 12½" rectangle to the bottom of each unit from step 2. Press the seam allowances toward the new rectangle. Make four.

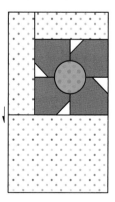

Make 2; make
2 reversed
(1 pink).

4. Sew a yellow polka-dot Flower block to one short edge of a white polka-dot 9½" x 12½" rectangle; press the seam allowances toward the rectangle. Make two with yellow polka-dot Flower blocks and two with yellow daisy-print Flower blocks.

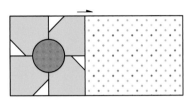

Make 2.

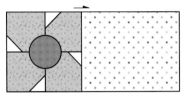

Make 2.

5. Using the photo on page 16 as a guide, sew a yellow unit to each raspberry or pink unit from step 3 to complete a corner unit. Make four; two will be mirror images of the others.

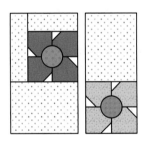

Make 2.

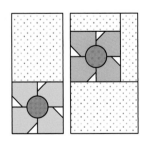

Make 2
(1 raspberry and 1 pink).

Flowerpot Blocks

1. Sew a Flowerpot block to the bottom of each Stem block. Press the seam allowances toward the Stem block.

2. Sew a unit from step 1 to each purple and orange Flower block. Press the seam allowances toward the stem units. Make four.

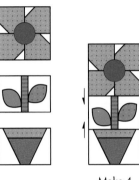

Make 4.

Borders

1. Beginning with a striped Awning block and alternating striped and dotted blocks, sew five Awning blocks together along their short edges. Be sure the white corners point in the same direction on each block. Make four.

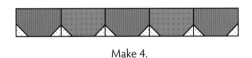

Make 4.

2. Sew a green large polka-dot 3½" x 5½" rectangle to each end of a border unit. Make two; these are the side borders.

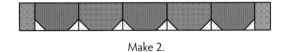

Make 2.

3. Sew a green large polka-dot 5½" x 8½" rectangle to each end of a remaining border unit. Make two; these are the top and bottom borders.

Make 2.

Assemble the Rows

1. Lay out the large corner sections, the Flowerpot sections, and the remaining pink Flower block as shown.

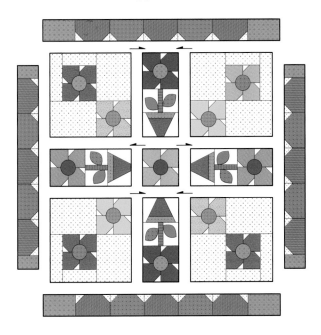

2. Sew the units together in rows. Press the seam allowances in each row toward the Flowerpot sections.
3. Sew side borders to the assembled unit. Attach the top and bottom borders to complete the quilt top.

Finish the Quilt

1. Cut the backing fabric into two 65" lengths. Remove the selvages and sew the two sections together along one long edge. Layer the quilt top, batting, and backing and baste the layers together.
2. Quilt as desired.
3. Trim the backing and batting to match the quilt top, squaring the corners.
4. From the binding fabric, cut enough 2¼"-wide bias strips to equal 280".
5. Bind the edges as detailed in "Binding" (page 94).

Strawberry Flowerpot

A friend shared this idea, but not its source, with me. It makes a fun, edible centerpiece that adds a touch of whimsy to a quilting luncheon.

INGREDIENTS

1 head romaine lettuce
12 big strawberries
12 miniature marshmallows
12 wooden skewers
1 flowerpot or watering can

Wash and dry the head of lettuce, keeping it intact. Place the lettuce upright in the flowerpot; it should fit snugly in the flowerpot to stay in place. Wash and dry the strawberries, leaving the stems on. Cut an X in the pointed end of each berry and open the berry slightly. With the berry's cut end facing up, insert a skewer from the stem end and through the berry, ending about ½" beyond the berry top. Add a miniature marshmallow to the top of the skewer. Stick the bottom ends of the skewers into the head of lettuce, varying the skewer heights, to make an edible arrangement of strawberry flowers.

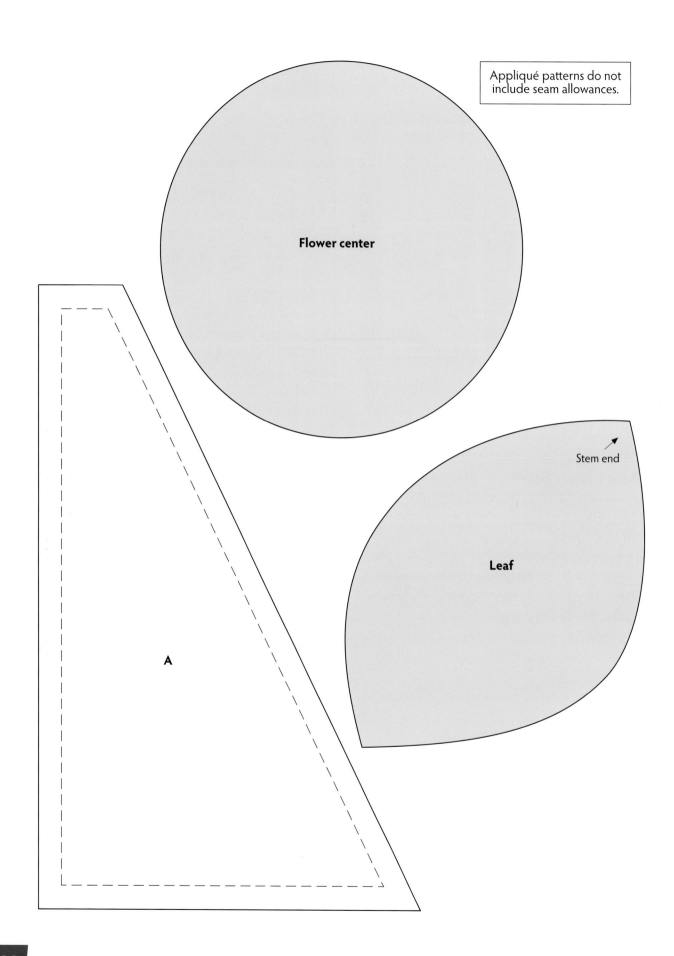

Appliqué patterns do not include seam allowances.

Flower center

Stem end

Leaf

A

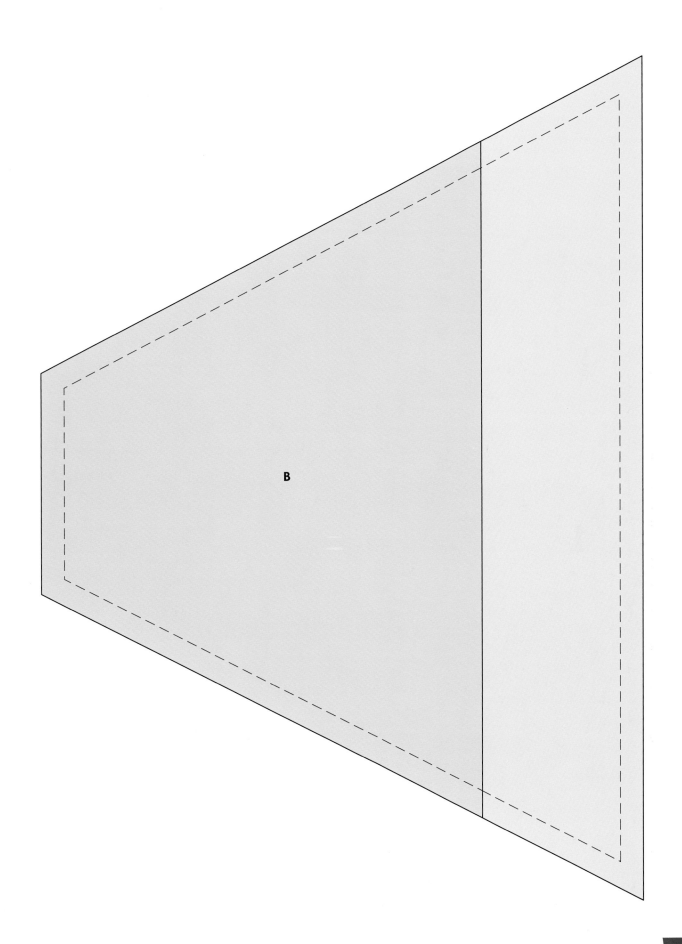

B

Petits Fours

Pieced and appliquéd by Barbara Jones; quilted by Sue McCarty

Finished quilt: 70" x 80"

FINISHED BLOCKS:

Large Four Patch blocks: 6" x 6" • **Small Four Patch blocks:** 4" x 4"

Rose blocks: 10" x 20"

Named for those dainty little cakes iced in pastel frosting and decorated with tiny flowers, this quilt is just as yummy— but it's calorie-free! It's easy to make with two sizes of Four Patch blocks and just a touch of appliqué. If appliqué isn't your cup of tea, you can omit it and simply make a few more large and small Four Patch blocks to fill in the gaps.

Materials

Yardage is based on 42"-wide fabric.

2⅓ yards of floral-striped fabric for outer border

1¾ yards *total* of assorted pink, yellow, green, off-white, red, and salmon scraps (at least 4" wide)

1½ yards of off-white print for sashing

⅔ yard of light-pink paisley for appliqué background

½ yard of salmon pindot for inner border

¼ yard of red tone-on-tone print for roses

⅛ yard *each* of 3 assorted green prints for leaves

⅛ yard of pink-and-yellow striped fabric for rose centers and leaves

¾ yard of salmon paisley for binding

4¾ yards of fabric for backing

74" x 84" piece of batting

Basic appliqué tool kit (see page 6)

Cutting

Appliqué patterns are on page 28. Cutting for all patchwork pieces includes ¼" seam allowances.

From the floral-striped fabric, cut on the lengthwise grain:*

4 strips, 6" x length of fabric

**You can use leftovers from the floral-striped fabric to cut squares for the Four Patch blocks, if desired.*

From the assorted scraps, cut:*

144 squares, 3½" x 3½"

96 squares, 2½" x 2½"

**You can use leftovers from the floral-striped fabric to cut squares for the Four Patch blocks, if desired.*

From the off-white print, cut:

8 strips, 6½" x 42"; crosscut into 59 rectangles, 4½" x 6½"

From the light-pink paisley, cut:

3 rectangles, 11½" x 21½"

From the salmon pindot, cut:

7 strips, 2" x 42"

From the red tone-on-tone print, cut:

9 using rose-petal pattern

From the assorted green prints, cut:

12 using assorted leaf patterns

From the pink-and-yellow striped fabric, cut:

3 using flower-center pattern

3 using assorted leaf patterns

Make the Four Patch Blocks

1. Sew assorted 3½" squares together in pairs. Press the seam allowances to one side. Sew the pairs together to complete 36 Large Four Patch blocks.

Large Four Patch.
Make 36.

2. Sew assorted 2½" squares together in pairs. Press the seam allowances to one side. Sew the pairs together to complete 24 Small Four Patch blocks.

Small Four Patch.
Make 24.

Appliqué the Rose Blocks

1. Prepare the appliqué shapes and baste, glue baste, or pin in place on the light-pink paisley rectangles, referring to the photograph for placement.

2. Appliqué the pieces to the background fabric. Press the block, and then trim to 10½" x 20½", centering the appliqué. Make three Rose blocks.

Assemble the Quilt Top

This quilt top is assembled in rows, but you may want to lay out all blocks before sewing to ensure you're happy with the color placement of the scrappy blocks.

1. For each large Four Patch row, lay out six blocks and five off-white sashing rectangles. Sew the pieces together to complete the row. Press the seam allowances toward the sashing pieces. Make four rows.

Large Four Patch row.
Make 4.

2. For each small Four Patch row, use six sashing rectangles and five blocks. Sew the pieces together and press the seam allowances toward the sashing pieces. Make three rows.

Small Four Patch row.
Make 3.

3. For the Rose-block rows, the remaining Four Patch blocks and sashing strips are assembled into short rows before adding the appliquéd blocks. Join four large Four Patch blocks and three sashing pieces. Then assemble four sashing rectangles with three small Four Patch blocks. Sew the large Four Patch row to the bottom edge of the small Four Patch row. Make two.

4. Sew a completed appliquéd Rose block to the left end of one unit from step 3 to make row 2. Attach a second appliquéd block to the right end of a second step 3 unit to assemble row 5.

Make 1 of each.

5. To make row 4, join two large Four Patch blocks and two sashing pieces. Sew together two small Four Patch blocks and two sashing pieces; sew to the upper edge of the large Four Patch short row. Make a second unit with two large Four Patch blocks and one sashing piece attached to a short row containing one small Four Patch block and two sashing pieces. Sew the wider unit to the left edge of the remaining Rose block and the narrower unit to the appliquéd block's right edge. Press the seam allowances toward the Rose block.

Make 1.

6. Join the rows as shown. Press.

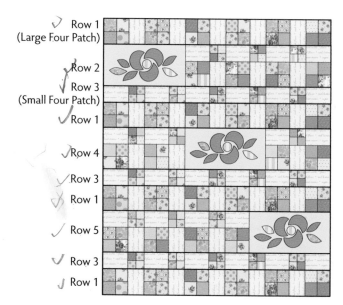

Quilt layout

Add the Borders

In the quilt shown, I added the inner salmon border with butted corners, but mitered the floral-striped border.

1. Sew the salmon 2"-wide strips together end to end to make a continuous strip.

2. Measure the length of the quilt top (it should be 66½") and use this measurement to cut two lengths from the long salmon strip. Sew these strips to the sides of the quilt and press the seam allowances toward the strips.

3. Measure the width of the quilt, including borders (it should be 59½"), and cut two salmon strips to this length. Sew them to the top and bottom of the quilt top and press.

4. For the outer border, center a floral-striped 6"-wide strip along one side of the quilt top. The ends of the strip will extend beyond the ends of the quilt top; *do not trim them!* Sew the strip to the quilt, beginning and ending ¼" from each edge of the quilt top and backstitching at each end. Finger-press the borders away from the quilt center. Repeat for all four sides of the quilt.

5. Overlap the borders as shown. On the wrong side, mark a 45° diagonal line on the border fabric that starts at the point where you stopped stitching (¼" from the edge of the quilt top). The line should run to the outside edge of the border. This will be your stitching line. Mark both ends of each border strip in this manner.

6. Miter the corners as follows. Working on one corner at a time, place the two border strips right sides together, matching the marked sewing lines; pin. Sew the seam, starting at the inner corner by the quilt top and stitching toward the outer edge of the border strips. Press the seam allowances open. Check from the right side of the quilt top to make sure everything is lying flat and not puckered or tucked. Once you're satisfied with a smooth corner, trim the excess border fabric, leaving ¼" seam allowances. Repeat for all corners.

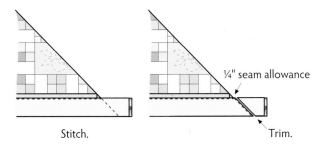

Stitch.   ¼" seam allowance   Trim.

Finish the Quilt

1. Prepare the backing fabric so that it's approximately 4" larger than the quilt top in both directions. Layer the quilt top, batting, and backing and baste the layers together.

2. Quilt as desired.

3. Trim the backing and batting to match the quilt top, squaring the corners.

4. From the binding fabric, cut enough 2¼"-wide bias strips to equal 340".

5. Bind the edges as detailed in "Binding" (page 94).

Petits Fours

INGREDIENTS

2 pound cakes (homemade or purchased), cut into desired shapes such as small rectangles, diamonds, or squares
2 pounds confectioner's sugar
¼ cup butter, melted
1 teaspoon almond or vanilla extract
1 cup light cream
Food coloring
Sprinkles, coconut, candied cherries, chopped nuts, or other desired toppings for decorating

Set cake and toppings aside and place all other ingredients in the top of a double boiler over hot water. Stir until smooth. Divide frosting into several small bowls, one for each desired color, and add food coloring to each.

Spear each piece of cake with a skewer and dip into frosting. Remove and twirl so frosting covers evenly. Place on waxed paper to cool. Decorate as desired with sprinkles or other toppings.

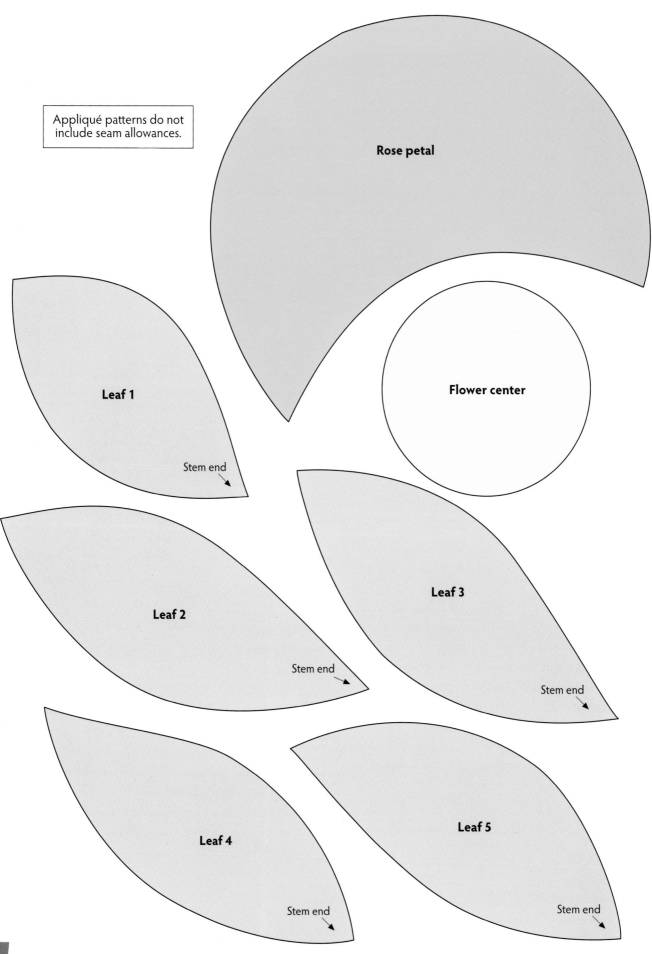

Appliqué patterns do not include seam allowances.

Rose petal

Leaf 1

Flower center

Stem end

Leaf 2

Leaf 3

Stem end

Stem end

Leaf 4

Leaf 5

Stem end

Stem end

Social Networking

Appliquéd and pieced by Barbara Jones; quilted by Catherine Timmons

Finished quilt: 63" x 79"

I am guilty of it and you might be, too. When I want to show how excited I am on my blog or in my written patterns, I add about 7,000 exclamation points to the end of a sentence! When I want to indicate that a story will be continued or that I will be right back, I use an ellipsis . . . Of course, asterisks still mean see the note or fine print. I thought this quilt would be the perfect place to use fabrics printed with words and letters, with a stripe or two thrown in for good measure. Whichever fabrics you choose, the appliquéd punctuation will get your message across.

Materials

Yardage is based on 42"-wide fabric.

2½ yards of black graphic print for blocks, border, and binding

⅞ yard of sage squiggle print for appliqué backgrounds

⅞ yard of sage graphic print for appliqué and pieced blocks

⅞ yard of white squiggle print for appliqué and pieced blocks

⅞ yard of black striped fabric for appliqué and pieced blocks

¾ yard of black small-scale print for appliqué and pieced blocks

⅝ yard of large-white-dots-on-black print for pieced blocks

⅝ yard of cream tone-on-tone fabric for appliqué and pieced blocks

½ yard of sage small-scale print for appliqué and pieced blocks

⅓ yard of sage striped fabric for appliqué and pieced blocks

¼ yard of black squiggle print for appliqué and pieced blocks

⅛ yard of large-black-dots-on-white print for appliqué and pieced blocks

4 yards of fabric for backing

67" x 83" piece of batting

Template plastic

Basic appliqué tool kit (see page 6)

Cutting

Appliqué patterns are on pages 35 and 36. Cutting for all patchwork pieces includes ¼" seam allowances.

From the black graphic print, cut *on the lengthwise grain:*

1 rectangle, 2½" x 71½"

1 rectangle, 5" x 63½"

1 rectangle, 4" x 63½"

1 rectangle, 3½" x 60½"

1 rectangle, 10½" x 25½"

From the sage squiggle print, cut:

1 rectangle, 13½" x 25½"

1 rectangle, 11½" x 26½"

1 square, 7½" x 7½"

From the sage graphic print, cut:

1 rectangle, 12½" x 24½"

1 rectangle, 3½" x 12½"

1 rectangle, 11½" x 26½"

8 squares, 3½" x 3½"

From the white squiggle print, cut:

1 rectangle, 13½" x 25½"

1 rectangle, 2½" x 21½"

1 strip, 3½" x 42"; crosscut into 1 rectangle, 3½" x 15½", and 6 squares, 3½" x 3½"

1 *each* using patterns B and C

From the black striped fabric, cut:

1 strip, 2½" x 40½"

1 strip, 3½" x 33½"

2 strips, 2½" x 20½"

1 strip, 2½" x 18"

1 square, 13½" x 13½"

10 squares, 3½" x 3½"

3 using pattern A

1 using pattern B

12 using pattern D

From the black small-scale print, cut:

1 rectangle, 10½" x 25½"

1 rectangle, 6½" x 12½"

1 rectangle, 3½" x 24½"

1 rectangle, 2½" x 40½"

1 *each* using patterns B and C

From the large-white-dots-on-black print, cut:

1 rectangle, 11½" x 26½"

1 rectangle, 2½" x 40½"

2 strips, 3½" x 42"; crosscut into 6 squares, 3½" x 3½";

   1 rectangle, 3½" x 12½"; and 1 rectangle, 3½" x 9½"

From the cream tone-on-tone fabric, cut:

1 rectangle, 11½" x 26½"

4 rectangles, 1½" x 42"

6 squares, 3½" x 3½"

6 using pattern D

From the sage small-scale print, cut:

1 rectangle, 11½" x 26½"

1 square, 6½" x 6½"

4 squares, 3½" x 3½"

2 using pattern A

From the sage striped fabric, cut:

5 squares, 3½" x 3½"

1 *each* using patterns B and C

From the black squiggle print, cut:

1 rectangle, 3½" x 24½"

1 *each* using patterns B and C

From the large-black-dots-on-white print, cut:

1 strip, 2½" x 18"

3 using pattern E

Preparing the Pieced Circles

Two periods and the dot of one exclamation point are cut from pieced fabric for a half-and-half appearance.

1. Sew the 2½" x 18" strips together along one long edge. Press the seam allowances open.

2. Cut two circles using pattern A from this strip set, centering the template over the seam line. These are called half periods.

3. Cut one circle using pattern C from the strip set, centering the circle on the seam.

Make the Exclamation Point Panel

1. Each Exclamation Point block is made by appliquéing B and C patches to an 11½" x 26½" background. Position the C circle 3¾" above the lower edge of the background and centered from side to side. Center the B shape with its point ¾" above the circle.

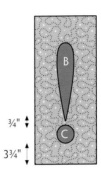

2. Begin with the sage squiggle-print background and the B and C patches cut from the black small-scale print. Glue baste the patches in place.

Uniform Placement Made Easy

For quick repeat placement on identical blocks, it's helpful to glue baste the patches of one block, and then use it as a guide. Place the block on a light table and lay the next background fabric on top of the basted block to position and glue baste its patches. Repeat for subsequent blocks. All the blocks will be the same without repeated measuring.

---

3. Appliqué both parts of the exclamation point to the background rectangle. Press. Repeat to appliqué the other Exclamation Point blocks using the photograph as a color-placement guide.

4. Trim each block to 10½" x 25½". Make five.

5. Sew the blocks together, adding the black graphic-print 10½" x 25½" rectangle as shown. The row will measure 25½" x 60½".

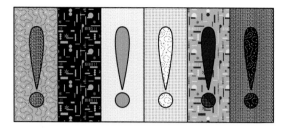

Exclamation Point panel

Make the Asterisk Panel

There are three Asterisk blocks and two blocks with only periods in this panel. All are appliquéd, pressed, and trimmed to size before they're sewn into two rows.

1. Center a half period on the sage squiggle-print 7½" square. Baste and stitch in place; press. Trim the block to 6½" x 6½".

2. For the rectangular Periods block, position two sage A circles 1½" above the lower edge of the small black print 10½" x 25½" rectangle. Place the first circle 1¾" from the right side of the rectangle and align the second circle so there will be approximately 2½" between the circles when they're complete. Baste, appliqué, and press. Trim the block to measure 9½" x 24½". Sew the 3½"-high black squiggle-print rectangle to the top of the appliquéd block. Press the seam allowances in either direction.

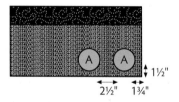

3. To make the square Asterisk block, position six D patches in a circle around the center of the black-striped 13½" square. Baste and stitch each shape in place; then baste and appliqué an E circle at the center. Because the circle will cover the points of the D patches, it isn't necessary to stitch perfect corners. Press the block and trim it to 12½" x 12½".

4. For one rectangular Asterisk block, position an asterisk (one E and six D pieces) and two A circles on a 13½" x 25½" rectangle, using the photo and illustrations as a placement guide. Position the asterisk approximately 1¼" from the left edge and 1¾" above the bottom, with the right circle 1¼" from the right raw edge. The second circle is approximately 2½" from the right circle and 4" from the asterisk when finished. Align the lower edges of the circles with the bottom of the asterisk. Repeat to make a second block, replacing one of the A circles with a pieced circle. Glue baste and appliqué the blocks; press. Trim each block to measure 12½" x 24½".

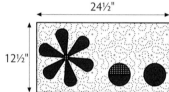

5. Sew the sage small-scale print 6½" square to the right side of the block from step 1. Press the seam allowances away from the appliquéd block. Sew the black small-scale print 6½" x 12½" rectangle to the top of the assembled unit. Press the seam allowances toward the large rectangle.

6. Sew the Periods block from step 2 between the rectangular and square Asterisk blocks as shown. Press the seam allowances toward the Asterisk blocks. This row measures 12½" x 60½".

7. Join the sage graphic-print 12½" x 24½" rectangle, the remaining Asterisk block, and the unit from step 5 to make the bottom half of the panel. Press the seam allowances toward the Asterisk block. This row also measures 12½" x 60½".

8. Sew the two rows together and press the seam allowances in either direction to create a 24½" x 60½" panel.

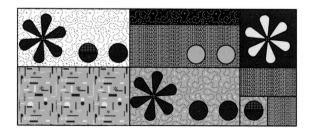

Make the Center Pieced Panel

This panel contains three sashing strips and two pieced rows. The rows and sashes are assembled first, and then joined to create the panel.

Sashing Strips

1. Sew a black striped 2½" x 20½" rectangle to the left end of the black small-scale print 2½" x 40½" rectangle. Press the seam allowances toward the striped fabric. This is the top sashing strip.

2. To make the bottom sashing strip, sew the black striped 2½"-wide rectangles together along one short edge. Press the seam allowances in either direction.

Pieced Rows

1. Sew four sage graphic-print 3½" squares to four white squiggle-print squares and press the seam allowances toward the sage squares. Sew the sage graphic-print 3½" x 12½" rectangle to the white square at the left end of the strip. Stitch the white squiggle-print 3½" x 15½" rectangle to the sage square at the right end, and then join the large-white-dots-on-black 3½" x 9½" rectangle to the white rectangle to complete the unit.

2. Stitch four sage small-scale print, one white squiggle-print, four sage graphic-print, and seven cream tone-on-tone 3½" squares together as shown below. Press as shown. Sew the large-white-dots-on-black 3½" x 12½" rectangle to the sage square at the left end of the strip to complete the unit.

3. Sew the units from steps 1 and 2 together to make row 1. The row should measure 6½" x 60½".

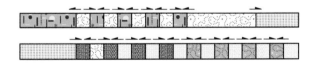

4. Sew five sage striped 3½" squares to four black striped squares as shown, with sage squares at both ends of the strip. Stitch the black striped 3½" x 33½" rectangle to the left end of the strip.

5. Join six white-dots-on-black 3½" squares and six black striped squares to make a strip. Sew the black small print 3½" x 24½" rectangle to the right end of the unit.

6. Stitch the step 4 and 5 strips together as shown to make row 2, measuring 6½" x 60½".

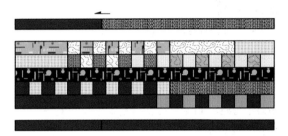

7. Sew the black graphic-print 3½" x 60½" strip between rows 1 and 2. Press the seam allowances toward the black strip. Attach the top and bottom sashing strips to complete the center panel, which measures 19½" x 60½".

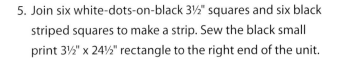

Assemble the Quilt Top

1. Sew the Exclamation Point panel to the top of the pieced center panel. Press the seam allowances toward the top sashing strip.

2. Sew the Asterisk panel to the bottom of the center pieced panel and press the seam allowances toward the bottom sashing strip.

3. Remove the selvages from the cream tone-on-tone 1½"-wide strips and join the strips end to end, creating one continuous piece. From the strip, cut one 68½" length for the left inner border and one 61½" length for the top inner border.

4. Sew the left inner border to the left side of the quilt unit. Add the inner border to the top edge of the quilt. Press the seam allowances toward the border strips.

5. Sew the large-white-dots-on-black and white squiggle-print 2½" rectangles together at one short end and press the seam allowances in either direction. Sew the strip to the quilt's lower edge, with the dotted fabric on the left.

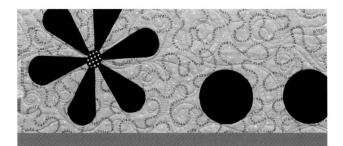

6. Attach the black graphic-print 71½" rectangle to the quilt's left side and press the seam allowances toward the rectangle.

7. Sew the black graphic-print 4" x 63½" rectangle to the quilt's upper edge and the 5" x 63½" rectangle to the lower edge. Press the seam allowances toward the black rectangles.

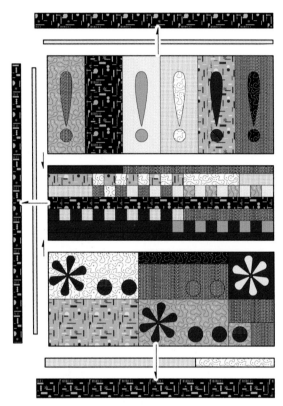

Quilt layout

Finish the Quilt

1. Remove the selvages from the backing fabric and cut it into two 65" lengths. Sew the pieces together along one long edge. Press the seam allowances in either direction.

2. Layer the quilt top, batting, and backing and baste the layers together.

3. Quilt as desired.

4. Trim the backing and batting to match the quilt top, squaring the corners.

5. From the binding fabric, cut enough 2¼"-wide bias strips to equal 325".

6. Bind the edges as detailed in "Binding" (page 94).

Sage and Sausage Risotto

INGREDIENTS

1 Tablespoon olive oil

1 pound sausage (Italian, chicken, or turkey)

1 onion, chopped

1 clove garlic, minced

½ teaspoon dried thyme

½ teaspoon dried ground sage

1¼ cups Arborio rice

1 cup chardonnay or other dry white wine

3½ cups low-sodium chicken broth

1 cup frozen tiny sweet peas or chopped broccoli

¼ cup grated parmesan cheese

Chopped fresh parsley for garnish

Heat oil in a heavy Dutch oven or large saucepan. Sauté sausage and onion until onion is translucent, about 10 minutes. Drain excess oil. Add garlic, thyme, and sage and cook about 30 seconds. Add rice and wine. Stir 1 to 2 minutes until wine is absorbed.

Stir in chicken broth. Lower heat to medium-low and simmer, uncovered, until broth is absorbed, stirring occasionally, about 15 minutes. Continue adding stock, ¼ cup at a time, and stirring until the liquid is absorbed and the rice is tender and creamy, about 5 minutes. Stir in peas or broccoli and ¼ cup parmesan. Cook for 1 minute or until heated through. Season to taste. Garnish with extra parmesan and chopped fresh parsley if desired. Serve immediately.

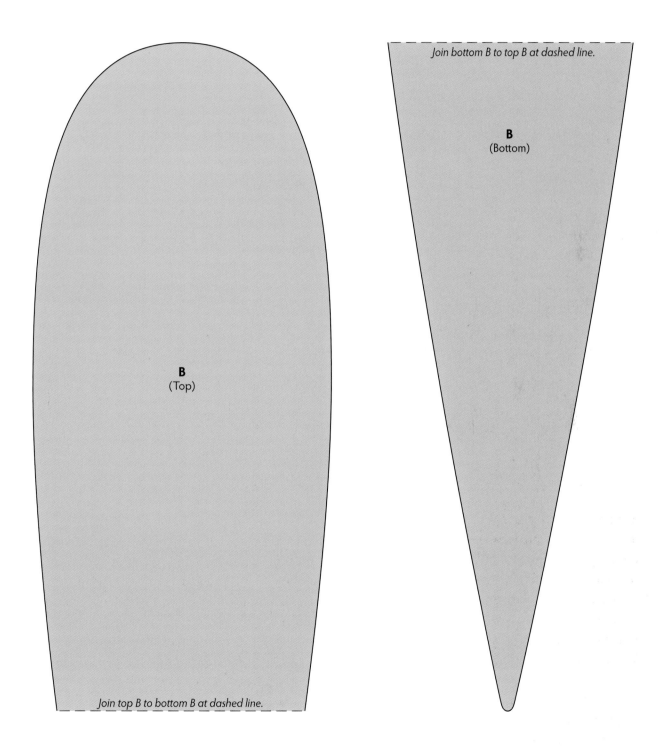

Patterns do not include seam allowances.

B
(Top)

Join top B to bottom B at dashed line.

Join bottom B to top B at dashed line.

B
(Bottom)

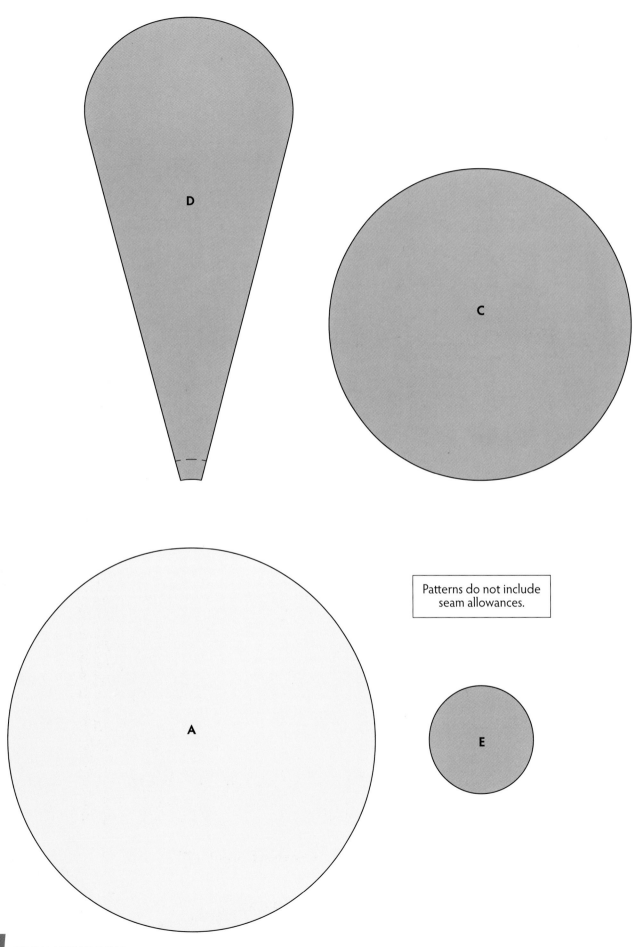

Patterns do not include
seam allowances.

Cherry Cioppino

Appliquéd and pieced by Barbara Jones; quilted by Catherine Timmons

Finished quilt: 50¾" x 68" • **Finished blocks:** 9" x 16"

Cioppino (cha-PEE-no) is an Italian seafood stew that's made in coastal towns where seafood is plentiful. It came to America via the wharves in San Francisco. Legend has it that someone would have a pot of soup cooking and all the fishermen who came by would contribute some of whatever they had just caught. The soup was left to simmer all day as ingredients were added; at dinnertime, it was served to all who had contributed.

This quilt has an eclectic look, as if several people contributed the fabrics that went into the quilt. It would be fun to host a quilting day where everyone donated a fat quarter, got together to sew the blocks, and finished the day with a bowl of cioppino. The piecing is simple. I recommend this pattern for any of today's large-scale prints or any collection that you're dying to work with.

Materials

Yardage is based on 42"-wide fabric.

1⅞ yards of red medium-scale print for borders and blocks

⅞ yard of multicolored striped fabric for sashing

¾ yard of black print for borders, sashing, and blocks

⅓ yard of yellow medium-scale print for blocks

⅓ yard of pink paisley for blocks

¼ yard *each* of large cherry print, red-with-white print, green-and-white print, light-pink floral, green paisley, and red solid for blocks

¼ yard of black tone-on-tone fabric for posts and blocks

⅛ yard of gray-and-white print for blocks

⅛ yard of light-green floral for blocks

½ yard of fabric for binding (see "Binding Option" below)

3¼ yards of fabric for backing

55" x 73" piece of batting

Template plastic

Binding Option
You will have enough of the red medium-scale print, after cutting the borders and blocks, to make the binding strips for the quilt. Purchasing an additional, contrasting ½ yard of fabric for binding is optional.

Cutting

Cutting for all patchwork pieces includes ¼" seam allowances.

From the red medium-scale print, cut:

1 *lengthwise* strip, 5¾" x 65½" (see "Border Lines" opposite)

1 *lengthwise* strip, 3" x 51¼"

2 strips, 3½" x 42"; crosscut into 4 rectangles, 3½" x 8½", and 4 rectangles, 3½" x 4½"

From the multicolored striped fabric, cut:

1 strip, 12½" x 42"; crosscut into 15 rectangles, 2" x 12½"

1 strip, 11" x 42"; crosscut into 10 rectangles, 2" x 11"

8 rectangles, 1½" x 9½"

From the black print, cut:

4 strips, 2½" x 42"

1 strip, 9½" x 42"; crosscut into 20 rectangles, 1½" x 9½"

1 strip, 3½" x 42"; crosscut into 2 rectangles, 3½" x 8½", and 2 rectangles, 3½" x 4½"

From the yellow medium-scale print, cut:

3 strips, 3½" x 42"; crosscut into 8 rectangles, 3½" x 8½", and 7 rectangles, 3½" x 4½"

From the pink paisley, cut:

3 strips, 3½" x 42"; crosscut into 8 rectangles, 3½" x 8½", and 4 rectangles, 3½" x 4½"

From the large cherry print, cut:

2 strips, 3½" x 42"; crosscut into 4 rectangles, 3½" x 8½", and 8 rectangles, 3½" x 4½"

From the red-with-white print, cut:

2 strips, 3½" x 42"; crosscut into 6 rectangles, 3½" x 8½", and 3 rectangles, 3½" x 4½"

From the green-and-white print, cut:

2 strips, 3½" x 42"; crosscut into 6 rectangles, 3½" x 8½", and 4 rectangles, 3½" x 4½"

From the light-pink floral, cut:

2 strips, 3½" x 42"; crosscut into 6 rectangles, 3½" x 8½", and 4 rectangles, 3½" x 4½"

From the green paisley, cut:

2 strips, 3½" x 42"; crosscut into 4 rectangles, 3½" x 8½", and 4 rectangles, 3½" x 4½"

From the red solid, cut:

2 strips, 3½" x 42"; crosscut into 4 rectangles, 3½" x 8½", and 3 rectangles, 3½" x 4½"

From the black tone-on-tone fabric, cut:

2 strips, 2" x 42"; crosscut into 30 rectangles, 1½" x 2"

1 strip, 3½" x 42"; crosscut into 4 rectangles, 3½" x 4½"

From the gray-and-white print, cut:

1 strip, 3½" x 42"; crosscut into 2 rectangles, 3½" x 8½", and 4 rectangles, 3½" x 4½"

From the light-green floral, cut:

1 strip, 3½" x 42"; crosscut into 2 rectangles, 3½" x 8½", and 5 rectangles, 3½" x 4½"

Border Lines

Borders may be cut from the fabric length or width, depending on the pattern in the fabric. When the pattern is large and requires careful matching, I like to cut borders lengthwise to avoid seaming, although this generally requires more fabric. This was the case for the left and top borders of this quilt. I use the remaining fabric for binding or on the back of the quilt. If fabric pattern isn't a consideration, I cut borders widthwise and sew strips together to make the lengths needed, as I did for the right and bottom borders here.

Make the Blocks

This is a strip quilt made in columns. Each column is composed of three full blocks and one half block. All the blocks are pieced the same way and go together easily if you follow the pressing arrows in the illustrations.

Name That Patch

*For simplicity in the instructions, the rectangles cut from various fabrics are designated **large** (3½" x 8½") or **small** (3½" x 4½").*

Half Blocks

Within each half block are one small and two large rectangles cut from the same fabric, plus a contrasting small rectangle. The value of the three matching patches determines whether the half block is light or dark overall. Plan the placement of lights and darks in the blocks to give the quilt plenty of variety.

1. Sew a small light rectangle to a small dark rectangle at one short end and press the seam allowances toward the dark fabric.

2. Sew two large matching rectangles to the sides of the pieced unit and press the seam allowances toward the dark fabric. Make 14 light and 14 dark half blocks.

Make 14 of each.

Full Blocks

Sew a light half block to a dark half block as shown, with the contrasting rectangles adjoining, and press toward the light half. Make 12. You'll have two light and two dark half blocks left over to be placed at one end of the columns.

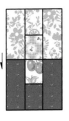

Make 12.

Assemble the Columns

1. Arrange the blocks and half blocks in columns as shown in the quilt assembly diagram. Sew black 1½" x 9½" rectangles between pairs of blocks. Press the seam allowances toward the black print. Stitch an additional black rectangle to each end of each column. Make four.

2. Sew striped 1½" x 9½" rectangles to the top and bottom of each column. Press the seam allowances toward the stripe.

Add the Vertical Sashing

There are two different striped rectangle lengths within each sashing strip. We'll call them "A" (2" x 11") and "B" (2" x 12½").

1. Sew a black tone-on-tone 1½" x 2" rectangle to one short end of an A rectangle and press the seam allowances toward the striped fabric. Make 10; this is unit A. Sew a second 1½" x 2" black rectangle to the opposite end of five of these units and press the seam allowances toward the striped fabric. These five are unit A+.

2. Stitch a black tone-on-tone 1½" x 2" rectangle to one short end of each B rectangle. Press the seam allowances toward the striped fabric. Make 15; this is unit B.

3. Sew sashing units together in this order: A, B, B, B, A+. Press the seam allowances toward the striped fabric. Make five.

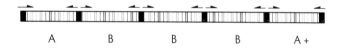

A   B   B   B   A +

Assemble the Quilt Top

1. Join the four block columns to the five vertical sashing strips as shown in the quilt diagram.

Border Dimensions

The border measurements given in the cutting instructions are the ideal. Measure your quilt top before making the final cuts.

2. Trim the selvages from all four black print 2½" x 42" strips. Sew two strips together along one short edge and press the seam allowances in one direction; make two. From one unit, cut a 2½" x 44" strip and sew it to the quilt's lower edge. Press the seam allowances toward the border.

3. Cut a 2½" x 65½" length from the remaining unit. Sew it to the right edge of the quilt top and press the seam allowances toward the border.

4. Sew the 65½"-long red strip to the left edge of the quilt. Press the seam allowances toward the border.

5. Sew the 51¼"-long red strip to the top of the quilt. Press the seam allowances toward the border.

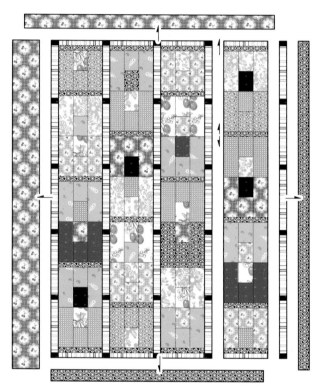

Quilt assembly

6. Using the patterns on pages 41 and 42, create a template for each border and corner curve section. Mark the curves with a pencil on the red borders before quilting, referring to "Curving the Borders" opposite. *Do not cut along the curved lines yet.*

Curving the Borders

Three templates are used to mark the curved edges of this quilt: corner template BT-1, left border template BT-2, and top border template BT-3. The straight edge of each template is designed to lie along the border seam line as an aid to proper placement.

1. Trace each of these patterns onto template plastic and cut out. Also mark the corner template with the dashed 45° line and label its top and left edges.

2. Position template BT-1 over the upper-left corner, with the dashed line bisecting the corner, and trace the curves. The corner where the curves meet does not align with the corner of the border pieces. Leave the corner template in place on the quilt.

3. Use the appropriate templates to mark the top and left borders. First position the appropriate template next to the corner template, abutting the template edges and aligning the curves, and trace the new curve. Next, slide the template along the quilt to the end of the traced curve and mark the next border section. Continue until the entire border length is marked.

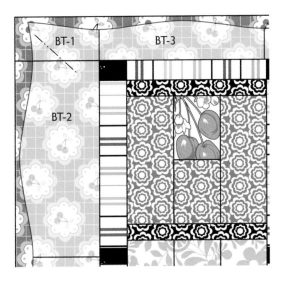

Finish the Quilt

1. Cut the backing fabric into two 55" lengths. Remove the selvages and sew the pieces together along one long edge.

2. Layer the backing, batting, and quilt top. Baste the layers together.

3. Quilt as desired. Trim the backing and batting even with the quilt top along the right and bottom edges. On the top and left sides, cut through all the layers along the marked curves.

4. From the binding fabric, cut enough 2¼"-wide bias strips to equal 280".

5. Bind the edges as detailed in "Binding" (page 94).

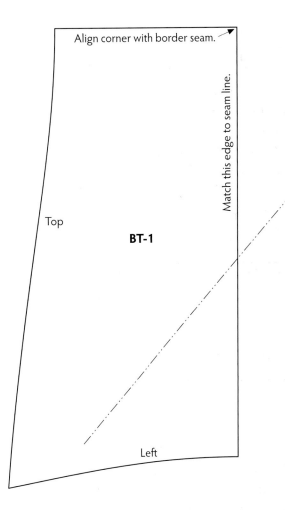

Align corner with border seam.

Match this edge to seam line.

Top

BT-1

Left

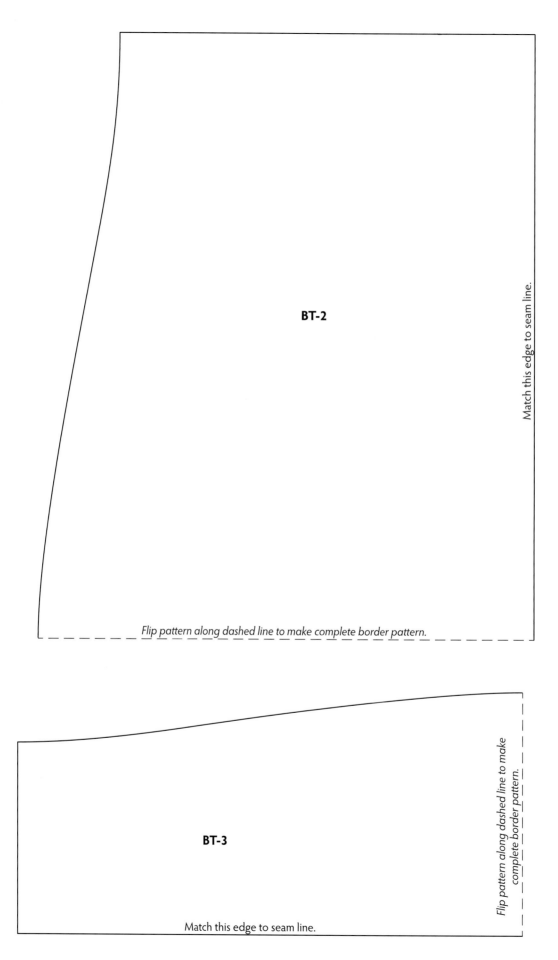

BT-2

Match this edge to seam line.

Flip pattern along dashed line to make complete border pattern.

BT-3

Flip pattern along dashed line to make complete border pattern.

Match this edge to seam line.

Summer Runner

Appliquéd and pieced by Barbara Jones;
quilted by Susan Wiley of Rose Garden Quilting

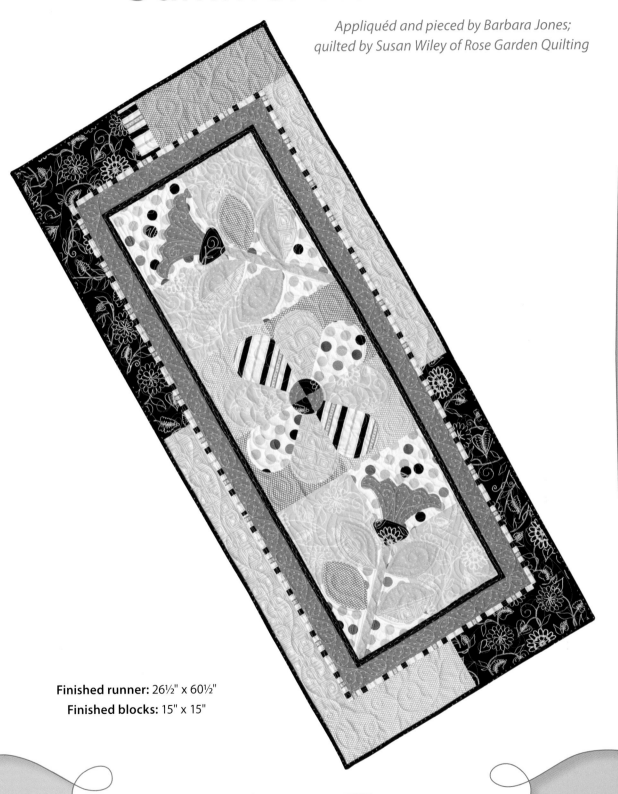

Finished runner: 26½" x 60½"
Finished blocks: 15" x 15"

This large table runner is perfect for a first-time needle-turn project. The appliqué is simple and minimal. Combine that with straightforward piecing, and a project doesn't get much easier! This runner features two different blocks—a Flower block and a Ring of Petals block. Once the blocks are sewn together in a row, they're surrounded by multiple colorful borders. If your table is small, simply vary the size of the runner by adding fewer borders.

Materials

Yardage is based on 42"-wide fabric.

⅝ yard of black tone-on-tone print for narrow inner border and binding

½ yard of red tone-on-tone print for flowers and second border

⅜ yard of black floral for appliqué and outer border

⅜ yard of blue floral for Flower blocks and center block petals

⅜ yard of white print for Flower blocks and center block petals

⅓ yard of black striped fabric for center block petals and third border

⅓ yard of light-green print for leaves, center block petals, and outer border

¼ yard of medium-green print for leaves and stems

¼ yard of peach print for center block and outer border

¼ yard of gray print for center block, leaves, and outer border

1⅔ yards of fabric for backing

30" x 64" piece of batting

Basic appliqué tool kit (see page 6)

Cutting

Cutting for all patchwork pieces includes ¼" seam allowances. For the best use of fabric, cut the largest pieces first. Appliqué patterns are on pages 48–50.

From the black tone-on-tone print, cut:

4 strips, 1" x 42"; crosscut 1 of these strips into 2 pieces, 1" x 15½"

Reserve the remaining fabric for binding.

From the red tone-on-tone print, cut:

4 strips, 2¼" x 42"; crosscut 1 of these strips into 2 pieces, 2¼" x 16½"

2 squares, 3" x 3"

2 using flower-head pattern

From the black floral, cut:

2 strips, 3½" x 22½"

1 strip, 5½" x 42"; crosscut into 1 strip, 5½" x 13", and 1 strip, 5½" x 11½"

2 squares, 3" x 3"

2 using calyx pattern

From the blue floral, cut:

1 strip, 8½" x 42"; crosscut into 4 squares, 8½" x 8½"

2 using pattern A

From the white print, cut:

1 strip, 8½" x 42"; crosscut into 2 squares, 8½" x 8½". From remainder of the strip, cut 2 squares, 8" x 8"; cut in half diagonally to yield 4 triangles.

2 using pattern B

From the black striped fabric, cut:

4 strips, 1" x 42"; crosscut 1 of these strips into 2 pieces, 1" x 20"

1 rectangle, 2" x 5½"

2 using pattern B

From the light-green print, cut:

2 strips, 3½" x 29"

1 strip, 2" x 42"

2 using pattern A

From the medium-green print, cut:

2 strips, 1½" x 14"

1 strip, 2" x 42"

1 using large leaf pattern

1 using small leaf pattern

From the peach print, cut:

2 squares, 8½" x 8½"

1 strip, 5½" x 14½"

From the gray print, cut:

2 squares, 8½" x 8½"

1 strip, 5½" x 14½"

1 using large leaf pattern

1 using small leaf pattern

Make the Flower Blocks

1. Find the center of each white triangle and each medium-green 14" strip by folding in half and finger-pressing.

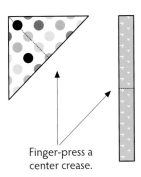

Finger-press a center crease.

2. Matching the centers and with right sides together, sew a green strip between two white triangles. Press the seam allowances toward the green strip. Using a ruler and rotary cutter, trim the block to measure 8½" square. Make two.

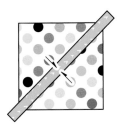 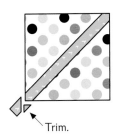

Trim.

3. Lay out the stem unit with one white and two blue-floral 8½" squares as shown. Making sure the stem is pointing toward the center of the unit, sew the squares together to make a four-patch unit. Make two.

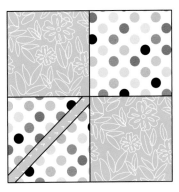

Make 2.

4. Sew together the light-green and medium-green 2"-wide strips. Press the seam allowances open. Align a large leaf template so the center of the leaf is on the seam line. Mark and cut out two large leaves. Repeat to make two small leaves.

Cut 2 large and 2 small leaves.

5. Position the appliqué pieces for the Flower blocks on the two four-patch units, referring to the quilt photo for placement. Pin, glue, or baste in place. Appliqué the pieces. Make two.

Make the Ring of Petals Block

1. Join two peach and two gray 8½" squares as shown to make a four-patch unit. Press the seam allowances open.

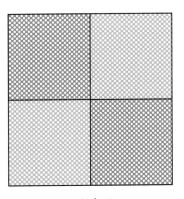

Make 1.

2. Sew the A and B petals together in pairs, matching the hash marks; they are mirror images, so be sure to sew them in the correct order. Sew the pairs of petals together to form a ring. Press the seam allowances open. Center the petal ring on the four-patch unit from step 1, aligning seams, and appliqué in place.

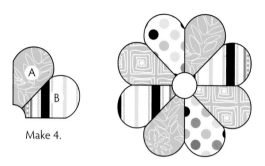

Make 4.

Join into ring.

Working with Petal Templates

- *Make two templates each from patterns A and B—one with seam allowances and one without.*
- *Use the templates with seam allowances to cut the patches. Either carefully cut the fabric along the template edges with a rotary cutter, or trace the template onto the wrong side of the fabric and cut with scissors just inside the traced outline. Transfer the hash marks to the fabric.*
- *Mark the sewing lines on each fabric patch by tracing around the templates without seam allowances.*

3. Sew the two red and two black 3" squares together into a small four-patch unit. Using the circle pattern (page 50), mark and cut one circle for the center of the petal ring. Appliqué in place.

Cut 1 circle.

4. Press and trim this block and the two Flower blocks to 15½" square. Take care to center the blocks when trimming by placing the 7¾" marks on the ruler along the background seam lines before cutting; the seam lines must align from one block to the next when you assemble the table runner.

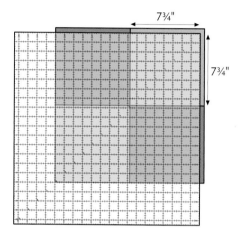

Trim blocks to 15½".
Each quadrant should be 7¾".

Assemble the Runner

1. Sew Flower blocks to opposite sides of the Ring of Petals block as shown. Press.
2. For the inner border, sew the black tone-on-tone 1" x 15½" strips to the short ends of the runner. Press the seam allowances toward the border strips. Sew the remaining black tone-on-tone 1"-wide strips together end to end. From this strip, cut two border strips, 46½" long, and sew them to the long sides of the runner. Press.
3. For the second border, sew the short red strips to the ends of the runner. Press the seam allowances toward the red strips. Join the remaining red strips end to end, and then cut two pieces, 50" long, from this strip and join them to the sides of the runner. Press.
4. For the third border, sew the black striped short strips to the ends of the runner. Press the seam allowances toward the red border. Join the remaining striped 1"-wide strips and from this long strip cut two pieces, 51" long. Join them to the sides of the runner. Press.
5. For the outer border, sew a light-green 3½" x 29" strip to a black floral 3½" x 22½" strip. Press the seam allowances toward the black strip. Make two and sew one to each long side of the runner, rotating them so that the color placement is opposite from one side to the

other. For the runner ends, sew the peach 5½" x 14½" strip to the black floral 5½" x 13" strip. Press the seam allowances toward the black floral and join to the bottom of the runner. Make the final border strip by joining the black floral 5½" x 11½" strip to the black striped 2" x 5½" rectangle. Join the gray 5½" x 14½" strip to the opposite side of the striped rectangle. Press the seam allowances toward the gray. Sew the border to the top of the table runner. Press.

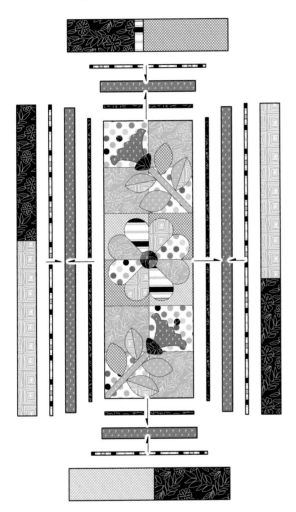

Finish the Runner

1. Trim the backing fabric to 31" x 65". Layer the quilt top, batting, and backing and baste the layers together.
2. Quilt as desired.
3. Trim the backing and batting to match the quilt top, squaring the corners.
4. From the black tone-on-tone print, cut enough 2¼"-wide bias strips to equal 205".
5. Bind the edges as detailed in "Binding" (page 94).

Creamy Raspberry Soup

This chilled berry soup is perfect for a summer luncheon.

INGREDIENTS

1½ Tablespoons unflavored gelatin
⅓ cup cold water
¾ cup hot water
¼ cup sugar
3 packages (10-ounce) frozen raspberries, thawed
1⅓ cups pineapple juice
1 cup half-and-half
⅓ cup grenadine
2 Tablespoons fresh lemon juice
3½ cups sour cream
1⅓ cups white wine, champagne, or white
    grape juice
Whole fresh berries and mint leaves for garnish

Soak gelatin in cold water for 5 minutes. Stir in hot water and sugar and dissolve over low heat; cool. Push thawed raspberries through a sieve to remove seeds. Combine with gelatin mixture. Stir in next 6 ingredients; puree. If you're using champagne, stir it in after you puree. Garnish with fresh whole berries and mint leaves.

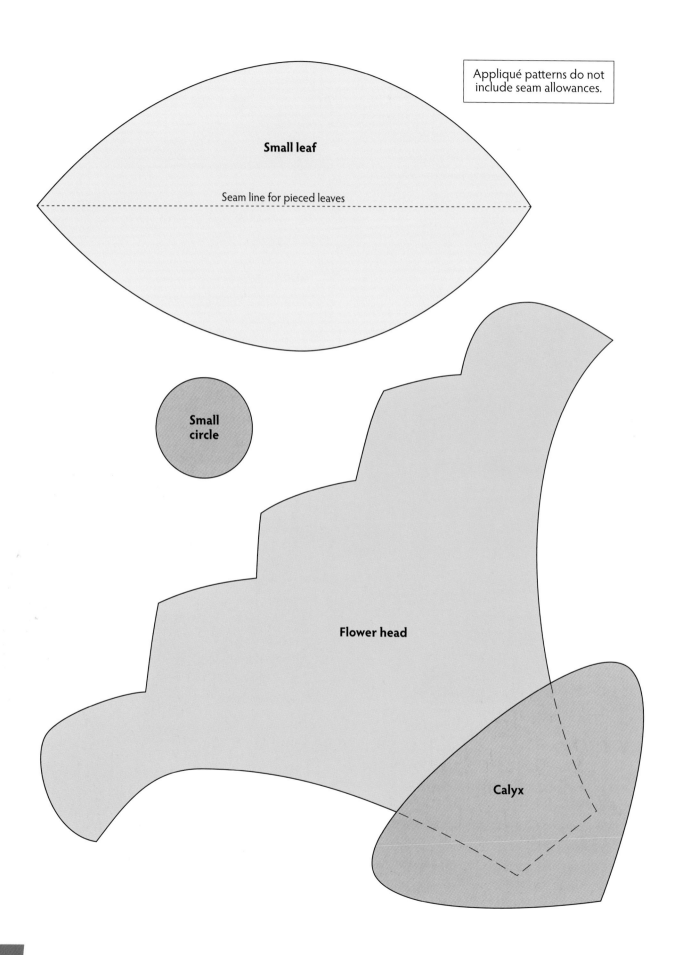

Appliqué patterns do not include seam allowances.

Small leaf

Seam line for pieced leaves

Small circle

Flower head

Calyx

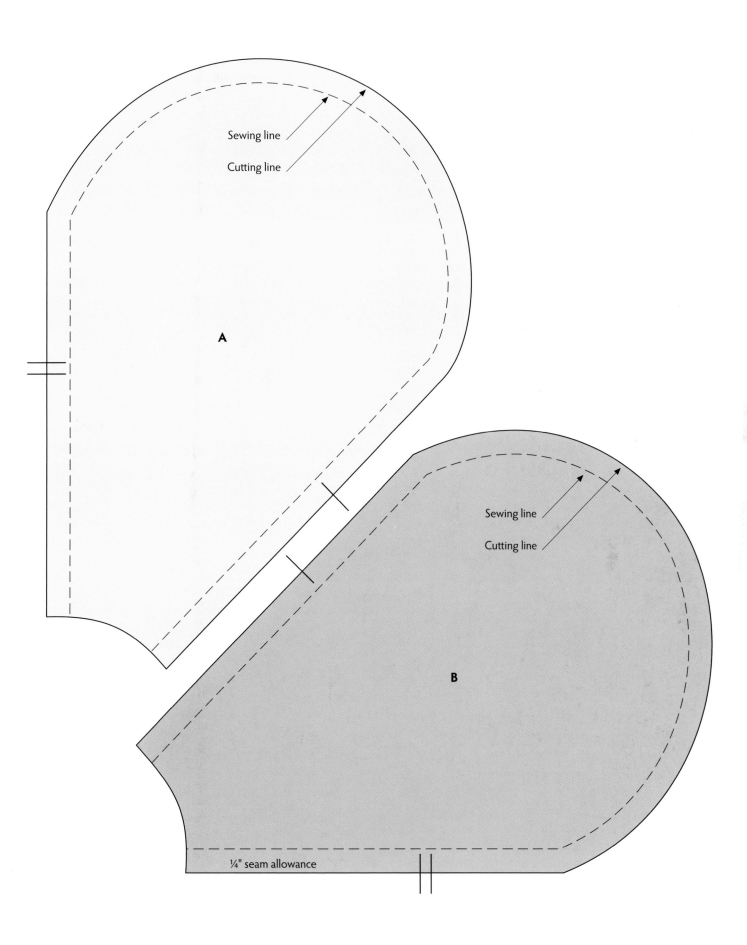

Sewing line

Cutting line

A

Sewing line

Cutting line

B

¼" seam allowance

Appliqué patterns do not include seam allowances.

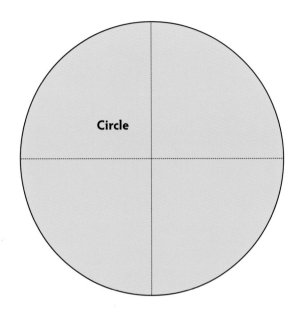

Circle

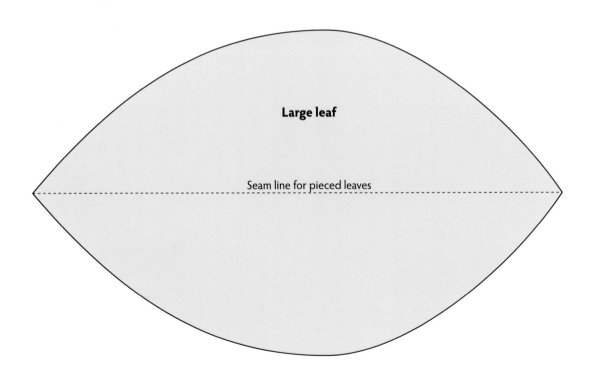

Large leaf

Seam line for pieced leaves

Seed Collectors

Appliquéd and pieced by Barbara Jones; quilted by Catherine Timmons

Finished quilt: 50" x 58"

I love texture, so brushed flannels and wools are two of my favorite fabrics to work with. Wool in particular is so easy to use. I secretly prefer working with solid colors, mum's the word on this, and wool is frequently solid in color. And brushed flannels offer the ultimate in coziness and touch-ability. I love to make a dark quilt from time to time as an homage to how we used to quilt.

Materials

Yardage is based on 42"-wide fabric.

1⅞ yards of blue-and-brown checked fabric for appliqué backgrounds, pieced blocks, and binding

1 yard of brown brushed flannel for flower backgrounds

½ yard of blue plaid for basket and pieced sashing

½ yard *total* of assorted green and yellow-green wools for leaves and flowers

⅓ yard of black print for pieced border

¼ yard of cream print for pieced blocks

¼ yard of brown print for sashing between flowers

¼ yard of blue wool for flowers

¼ yard of cream wool for flowers

¼ yard of dark-brown wool for birds

¼ yard of medium-brown plaid wool for birds

⅛ yard of green print for flower stems

⅛ yard of red-orange wool for flowers and seeds

⅛ yard *total* of assorted light yellow-green wools for leaves and stem

3 yards of fabric for backing

54" x 62" piece of batting

100% cotton thread to match basket fabric

1 skein *each* of blue, ivory, red, and brown embroidery floss to match patches

1 skein *each* of 3 different green embroidery flosses to match leaves

Freezer paper for templates

Size 7 embroidery needles

Basic appliqué tool kit (see page 6)

Template Time-Saver

I made appliqué templates from freezer paper for this quilt. Iron the freezer paper to the wool, and then cut around the template without adding a seam allowance. You can remove the template from the patch and reuse it, so you will only need to make one template for each appliqué in this quilt, i.e., one bird, one flower, one of each leaf template.

Cutting

Appliqué patterns are on pages 56–60. Cutting for all patchwork pieces includes ¼" seam allowances.

From the blue-and-brown checked fabric, cut:

1 *lengthwise* rectangle, 19½" x 51½"

1 *lengthwise* rectangle, 4½" x 41½"

1 *lengthwise* rectangle, 4½" x 23½"

1 rectangle, 2½" x 4½"

4 squares, 8" x 8"; cut twice diagonally to yield 16 triangles

From the brown brushed flannel, cut:

1 strip, 12" x 42"; crosscut into 2 squares, 12" x 12", and 1 rectangle, 12" x 13½"

1 strip, 21" x 42"; crosscut into 6 rectangles, 5¾" x 21"

From the blue plaid, cut:

1 strip, 3½" x 42"; crosscut into 4 squares, 3½" x 3½", and 7 squares, 2½" x 2½". Cut each 3½" square twice diagonally to yield 16 triangles.

1 each using patterns A and B

From the assorted green and yellow-green wools, cut:

3 *each* using patterns E, F, G, H, I, J, and K

2 using pattern L

1 using pattern D

From the black print, cut:

1 strip, 4½" x 42"; crosscut into 2 rectangles, 4½" x 9½", and 6 rectangles, 2½" x 3½"

2 strips, 2½" x 42"; crosscut into 2 rectangles, 2½" x 22½", 1 rectangle, 2½" x 4½", and 2 rectangles, 2½" x 3"

From the cream print, cut:

3 strips, 2⅛" x 42"; crosscut into 16 rectangles, 2⅛" x 5¼"

From the brown print, cut:

1 rectangle, 4½" x 30½"

1 strip, 2½" x 42"; crosscut into 1 rectangle, 2½" x 15½"; 1 rectangle, 2½" x 13½"; and 1 square, 2½" x 2½"

From the blue wool, cut:

3 using pattern L

1 using pattern Q

From the cream wool, cut:

5 using pattern M

From the dark-brown wool, cut:

1 *each* using patterns C and C reversed

1 using pattern Q

From the medium-brown plaid wool, cut:

1 using pattern C

2 using pattern C reversed

5 using pattern O

1 using pattern R

From the green print, cut:

2 strips, 1½" x 42"; crosscut into 3 rectangles, 1½" x 21"

From the red-orange wool, cut:

1 using pattern D

4 using pattern N

1 using pattern Q

From the light yellow-green wool, cut:

1 using pattern P

1 *each* using patterns H and J

Make the Blocks

Both pieced and appliquéd blocks are used in this quilt top. Start by piecing the backgrounds for the appliquéd designs.

Flower Blocks

1. Sew a green 1½"-wide rectangle between two brown flannel 5¾" x 21" rectangles. Press the seam allowances toward the green. Make three.

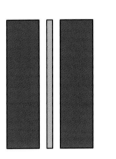

Make 3.

2. Arrange one each of patches H, I, J, and K around the green stem of one background unit. Glue baste the appliqués to the background and work a blanket stitch around the leaves; use two strands of the green embroidery floss that most closely matches the wool. Make three.

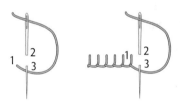

Blanket stitch

3. Sew brown brushed flannel 12" squares to the upper edge of two stem units. Attach the brown brushed flannel 12" x 13½" rectangle, oriented vertically, to the third stem unit. Position one each of patches E, F, G, L, M, N, and O on each of the new brown patches. Begin by placing the L patch so its lower edge slightly overlaps the seam between the background and the stem unit. Next, tuck the tips of patches E, F, and G underneath L, arranging them to overlap the stem as shown. Glue baste all the patches in place and repeat with the other two flower units. Blanket stitch each patch with two strands of matching embroidery floss.

4. Press and trim each block to measure 11½" wide, keeping the stem centered. Trim the two taller flowers (those with brown 12" background squares) to 30½" high, measuring up from the bottom of the stem. Trim the third flower unit to 30½" high, but measure down from the top of the unit and trim from the bottom of the stem unit.

5. Glue baste two each of patches D and Q and one R patch on the third flower unit near the bottom, as shown in the quilt photo. Blanket stitch around each patch with two strands of matching embroidery floss.

6. Sew a tall flower unit to the left edge of the third flower unit and press the seam allowances in either direction. Stitch the brown print 4½" x 30½" rectangle to the left edge of the remaining tall flower unit; press the seam allowances toward the brown print. Sew the two flower units together and press the seam allowances toward the brown print.

Basket Block

1. Position the basket (patches A and B) at the center of the blue-and-brown checked 19½" x 51½" rectangle, placing A about ⅞" up from the lower edge. Pin baste A and glue baste patch B; stitch patch B to the background.

2. Glue baste a green or yellow-green L piece to the background, at the right of the basket handle. Tilt the L patch to the right, using the dashed line on the pattern as a guide, and tuck it under A. Appliqué the basket to the background.

3. Glue baste patch P and the last L, H, and J patches in place; then glue baste all the remaining woolen patches. The left flower center uses a Q in place of the N patch. Blanket stitch each patch in place using two strands of matching embroidery floss.

4. Press and trim the block to 18½" x 50½".

Basket block.
Make 1.

Pieced Sashing Strip

1. For the top row, sew a black 2½" x 22½" rectangle to a brown 2½" x 15½" rectangle. Press the seam allowances toward the black.

2. To make the middle row, sew the six black 2½" x 3½" rectangles between seven blue plaid 2½" squares. Press the seam allowances toward the black fabric. Sew a black 2½" x 3" rectangle to each end of the pieced strip and press the seam allowances toward the black.

3. For the bottom row, stitch a brown 2½" x 13½" rectangle to a black 2½" x 22½" rectangle. Attach the 2½" brown square to the free end of the black rectangle. Press the seam allowances toward the black.

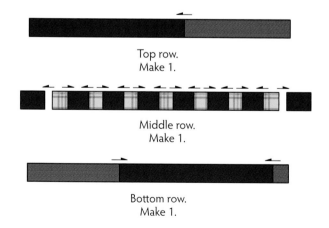

Top row.
Make 1.

Middle row.
Make 1.

Bottom row.
Make 1.

4. Sew the three rows together to complete the sashing strip.

Crisscross Blocks

1. Sew a blue plaid quarter-square triangle to one end of a 2⅛" x 5¼" cream rectangle. Make 16.

Make 16.

2. Attach a blue-and-brown checked quarter-square triangle to the shorter side of each unit. Press the seam allowances toward the checked fabric. Make 16.

Make 16.

3. Sew four units together into a block. Make four. The blocks should measure 9½" square.

Make 4.

Make a Match

As you join the Crisscross blocks, rotate every other block. The seam allowances will fall in opposite directions, making them easier to match.

Border Strips

1. Sew the blue-and-brown checked 2½" x 4½" rectangle between the black 2½" x 4½" rectangle and one 4½" x 9½" black rectangle. Press the seam allowances toward the checked fabric. Sew the assembled unit to one end of the 4½" x 23½" blue-and-brown rectangle; this is the left border.

2. Sew the blue-and-brown 4½" x 41½" rectangle to the remaining black 4½" x 9½" rectangle to make the top border. Press the seam allowances toward the black.

Assemble the Quilt

1. Sew the pieced sashing strip to the lower edge of the flower unit. Press the seam allowances away from the flower unit.

2. Sew the four Crisscross blocks into a column. Sew this column to the right edge of the flower/sashing unit.

3. Sew the left border to the left edge of the assembled unit. Stitch the top border to the upper edge.

4. Sew the basket panel to the bottom edge of the quilt. Press the seam allowances toward the basket block.

Quilt assembly

Finish the Quilt

1. Cut the quilt backing fabric into two 54" lengths. Remove the selvages and sew the two pieces together to make a rectangle about 54" x 80".

2. Layer the backing, batting, and quilt top. Baste the layers together.

3. Quilt the woolen patches minimally for a simpler look. The sample is echo quilted on the basket panel, with a loopy meander behind the flowers. Additional lines of quilting enhance the shapes of the appliqué patches.

4. Trim the backing and batting to match the quilt top.

5. From the binding fabric, cut enough 2¼"-wide bias strips to equal 250".

6. Bind the quilt, referring to "Binding" (page 94).

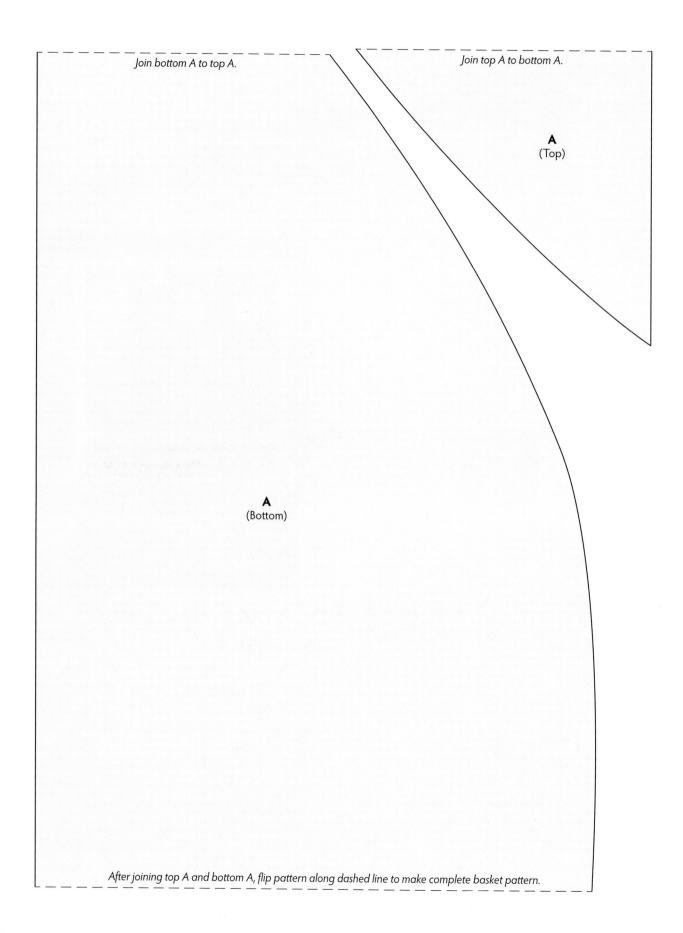

Join bottom A to top A.

Join top A to bottom A.

A
(Top)

A
(Bottom)

After joining top A and bottom A, flip pattern along dashed line to make complete basket pattern.

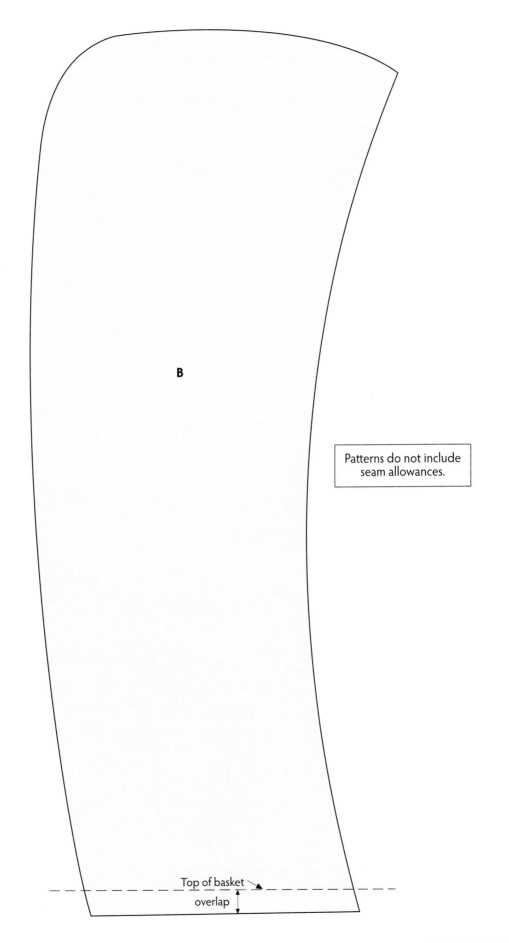

B

Patterns do not include
seam allowances.

Top of basket

overlap

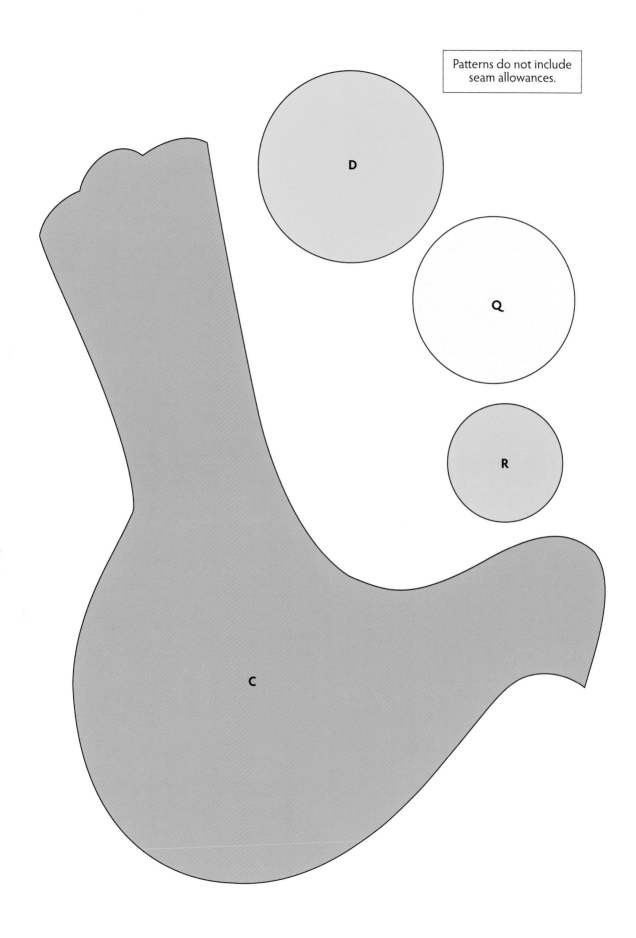

Patterns do not include seam allowances.

D

Q

R

C

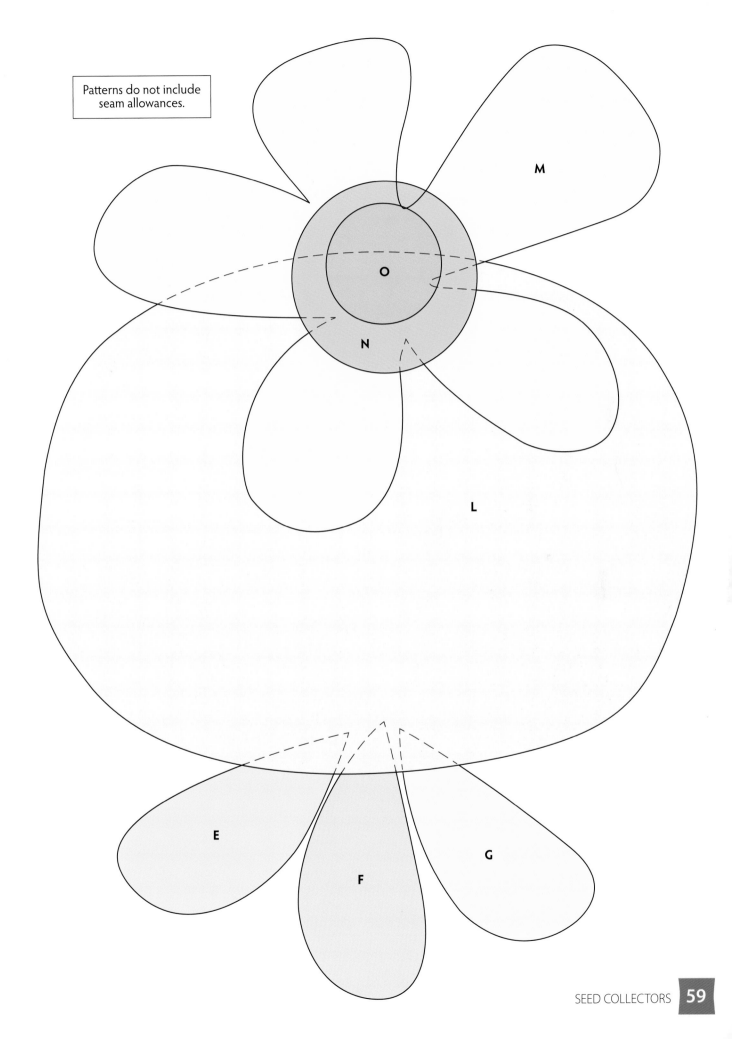

Patterns do not include seam allowances.

M

O

N

L

E

F

G

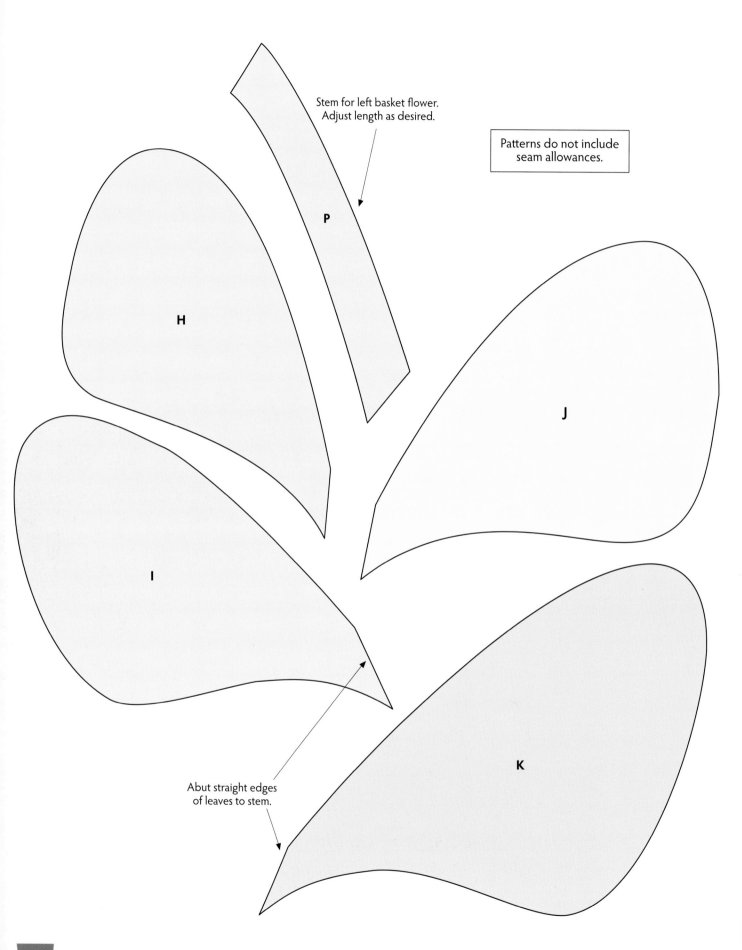

Stem for left basket flower.
Adjust length as desired.

P

Patterns do not include
seam allowances.

H

J

I

About straight edges
of leaves to stem.

K

Summer Cottage

Appliquéd and pieced by Barbara Jones; quilted by Catherine Timmons

Finished quilt: 76" x 76" • **Finished blocks:** 20" x 20"

I have a little summer cottage in Malad, Idaho, that used to belong to my father. On Memorial Day, or Decoration Day as the locals call it, cousins and friends return to Malad, so there's lots of visiting and catching up to do. Visitors drop by the house to chat, and we like to serve them a piece of cake. My grandpa grew rhubarb in his garden in Malad so the recipe for rhubarb upside-down cake, shared by Kathryn Lindsay, seemed like the right one to go with this quilt. It's one of the best I've ever eaten!

Materials

Yardage is based on 42"-wide fabric.

3 yards of off-white fabric for appliqué backgrounds

2¼ yards of yellow floral for outer border and House block borders

1⅞ yards of pink small plaid for inner border and binding

⅜ yard of pink-and-red striped fabric for roofs and flowers

⅜ yard of dark-peach fabric for heart vine, flowers, and window casings

⅓ yard of celery-green fabric for grass and appliqué

⅓ yard of pink large plaid for houses

¼ yard of small white floral for windows and flowers

1 fat quarter of red polka-dot fabric for pots and doors

1 fat quarter of light-pink plaid for Heart block

1 fat quarter *each* of 3 assorted green fabrics for leaves and stems

⅛ yard or scrap of light-peach floral for flowers

⅛ yard or scrap of light-peach solid for flowers

1 fat eighth *each* of 3 assorted blue fabrics for flowers and leaves

1 fat eighth of yellow plaid for leaves

1 fat eighth of dark-red floral for appliqué circles

4½ yards of fabric for backing

80" x 80" piece of batting

1 skein each of green and dark-rose embroidery floss

Basic appliqué tool kit (see page 6)

Cutting

Appliqué patterns are on pages 67–78. Cutting for all patchwork pieces includes ¼" seam allowances.

From the off-white fabric, cut:

3 strips, 21" x 42"; crosscut into 5 squares, 21" x 21"

2 strips, 17¼" x 42"; crosscut into 4 rectangles, 17¼" x 21"

From the yellow floral, cut:

2 *lengthwise* strips, 6½" x 76½"

2 *lengthwise* strips, 6½" x 64½"

8 strips, 3¼" x 42"; crosscut into 16 rectangles, 3¼" x 21".
  Cut 1 using pattern BH from each rectangle (16 total); see instructions.

3 using pattern U

1 using pattern AI

From the pink small plaid, cut:

2 *lengthwise* strips, 2½" x 64½"

2 *lengthwise* strips, 2½" x 60½"

1 using pattern AL

7 using pattern X

Reserve the remaining fabric for binding strips.

From the pink-and-red striped fabric, cut:

4 using pattern BG

From the dark-peach fabric, cut:

1 using pattern W

4 using pattern BB

8 using pattern BD

3 using pattern T

1 using pattern AH

From the celery-green fabric, cut:

2 strips, 4¼" x 42"; crosscut into 4 rectangles, 4¼" x 21"

From the pink large plaid, cut:

4 rectangles, 9¼" x 12" (AZ)

From the small white floral, cut:

8 using pattern BE

4 using pattern BC

3 using pattern H

From the red polka-dot fabric, cut:

4 *each* using patterns BA and BF

1 *each* using patterns K, V, AK, and AY

From the light-pink plaid, cut:

1 using pattern AA

From the assorted green fabrics, cut:

1 *each* using patterns A, A reversed, B, B reversed, C, D, D reversed, E, L, L reversed, M, M reversed, N, Q reversed, AB, AB reversed, AC, AC reversed, AD, AE, AE reversed, AF, AF reversed, AM, AN, AO, AP, AP reversed, AQ, AQ reversed, AR, AS, AT, AU, AV, AW, and AX

3 using pattern F

4 *each* using patterns J and Q

10 using pattern O

25 using pattern Z

6 using pattern AG

From the light-peach floral, cut:

2 using pattern R

From the light-peach solid, cut:

3 using pattern R

From the assorted blues, cut:

3 using pattern G from one fabric

1 *each* from a second fabric using patterns P and P reversed

3 from a third fabric using pattern P

3 using pattern Z

2 using pattern AG

From the yellow plaid, cut:

1 *each* using patterns E and F

2 using pattern O

2 using pattern Z

From the dark-red floral, cut:

3 using pattern I

5 using pattern S

8 using pattern Y

1 using pattern AJ

Make the Flower Blocks

Each of the Flower blocks is appliquéd to an off-white 21" background square. Position and glue baste all the patches for each block at least 1" inside the outer edge

of the background block using the drawings as a guide. Appliqué the patches in place following any special notes for the block. Press each block when the appliqué is complete and trim the block to 20½" square.

Top-Left Block

Pin baste the vase to the background to use as a guide for positioning the bottoms of the stems. Once the stems are in place, add the leaves and flowers. Glue baste all the pieces before you begin stitching to be certain of overall placement.

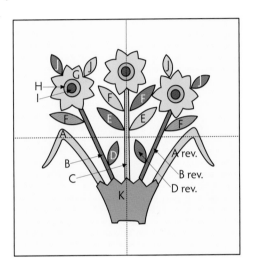

Top-Right Block

Pin baste the vase to the background and position the stems, tucking their lower ends under the top of the vase. Position the flowers and leaves. Glue baste all the pieces onto the background and stitch the appliqués.

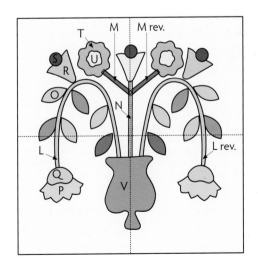

Center Block

Trace the word *Welcome* lightly in pencil on patch AA in the location shown. Center the heart on the background square and lightly glue baste in place.

Place patch W over the heart, making sure the inside edge of W covers the raw edge of AA by about ¼". Glue baste and appliqué the inside edge in place. Position, glue baste, and appliqué the other patches in the block. All the leaves are cut from pattern Z.

Embroider *Welcome* with a backstitch using three strands of rose embroidery floss.

All leaves are pattern Z.

Backstitch

Bottom-Left Block

Stitch the appliqué patches to the background block as before. Sew an AF patch to each AE patch using the unit appliqué method (page 13) before appliquéing the large leaves to the background.

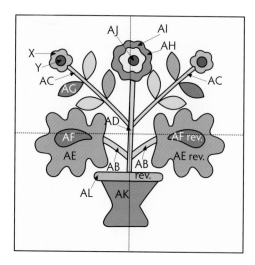

Bottom-Right Block

Glue baste and appliqué the patches to the background block. Trace the thin stems onto the background fabric and embroider with a stem stitch and three strands of green embroidery floss.

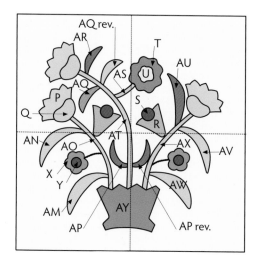

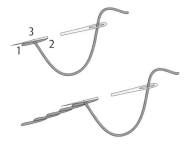

Stem stitch

Make the House Blocks

Each of the House blocks is constructed in the same way.

1. Sew a celery-green 4½" x 21" rectangle to the bottom of each off-white 17¼" x 21" rectangle. Press the seam allowances toward the green fabric.

2. Appliqué each window to the corresponding window frame. Trim the excess window-frame fabric from behind the window, leaving a ¼" seam allowance.

3. Position the windows and door on a house patch and stitch. Trim the excess house fabric from behind the windows and door.

4. Place the assembled house with its finished bottom edge along the seam in the background block. Baste and appliqué in place.

5. Position the roof at the top of the house. Tuck the chimney under the roof's upper edge as shown. Baste and appliqué both pieces.

6. Four BH appliqué patches create the scalloped border around each House block. The pattern includes appropriate allowances for seams and the oversized background fabric along the three straight edges. Trace the curved edge onto the fabric and add seam allowances for appliqué to the curved edge only. Matching the straight edges of the appliqués and background block, position and stitch the scalloped borders on the block sides. Place and appliqué borders at the top and bottom of the block, matching the straight edges and overlapping the side scalloped borders at the corners.

7. Make four House blocks. Press and trim each to 20½" square.

Assemble the Quilt

1. Sew a House block between the top-left and top-right blocks. Press the seam allowances away from the House block.

2. Sew the Heart block between two House blocks and press the seam allowances away from the House blocks.

3. Sew a House block between the bottom-left and bottom-right blocks. Press the seam allowances away from the House block.

4. Stitch the three rows of blocks together to make the quilt top.

5. Stitch a pink small plaid 2½" x 60½" strip to each side of the quilt. Press the seam allowances toward the border strips.

6. Attach the pink small plaid 2½" x 64½" strips to the quilt's top and bottom edges and press the seam allowances toward the border strips.

7. Sew the yellow floral 64½" strips to the quilt sides. Press the seam allowances toward the yellow borders.

8. Stitch the yellow floral 76½" strips to the quilt's top and bottom edges. Press the seam allowances toward the borders.

9. Using patterns BI and BJ (see "Border Templates," page 66), lightly mark the border scallops, beginning with the corners. The straight pattern edge aligns with the border seam line, and the short ends of the pattern pieces abut to create continuous curves. If it's necessary to adjust the scallop length to fit the quilt border, evenly distribute the difference along the entire border length. Do not cut the scalloped edge yet.

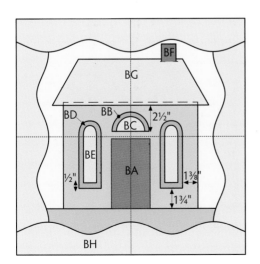

Border Templates

For the corner border template, begin with a 14" square of freezer paper. Fold it once on the diagonal and trace pattern BJ onto one half, matching the dashed line on the pattern to the freezer paper's fold. The peaks of the scallops will lie about ¼" from the paper edge. With the paper folded, cut along the wavy and straight edges, leaving the fold intact. Unfold to reveal the full corner template.

To make the side border template, cut a 6¼" x 48⅛" length of freezer paper and accordion fold it every 9⅝", making five sections. Trace pattern BI onto one section between folds, matching the straight edges. Cut the curved edge through all the freezer-paper layers and unfold.

When marking the quilt top, place this template on the quilt border between two marked corner sections. To adjust the scallops to fit, pinch out a portion of the excess length at each crease or slash and spread the template along the folds. Smooth the adjusted curves when tracing the curved edge onto the quilt top.

Finish the Quilt

1. Cut the quilt backing fabric into two equal lengths. Remove the selvages and sew the two pieces together to make a square about 80" x 80".
2. Layer the backing, batting, and quilt top. Baste the layers together.
3. Quilt as desired. Trim all the layers along the marked scallop edges.
4. Finish the quilt with bias binding using the leftover pink small plaid fabric; refer to "Binding" (page 94). Start at the peak of one scallop. Carefully pin the binding, without stretching it, around one scallop at a time and stitch. This job is best done without rushing. If the binding is stretched, the quilt edges will curl.

Rhubarb Upside-Down Cake

INGREDIENTS

⅔ cup boiling water
½ cup rolled oats (quick or slow-cooking)
½ teaspoon ground cinnamon
2 Tablespoons butter
⅓ cup sugar
2 cups diced rhubarb
1 cup flour
1 teaspoon baking powder
¼ teaspoon baking soda
¼ teaspoon salt
⅔ cup sugar
½ cup packed brown sugar
¼ cup cooking oil
1 egg
Fresh whipped cream, sweetened with sugar and vanilla

Pour boiling water over the rolled oats. Cover and let stand for 20 minutes. Meanwhile, place the butter in an 8" x 8" pan and heat in a 350° oven until melted. Stir in ⅓ cup sugar until dissolved. Add diced rhubarb, stir, and set aside.

Sift the dry ingredients together. In a large mixing bowl, combine ⅔ cup sugar, brown sugar, oil, and egg. Beat until combined. Add the oat mixture and beat well. Add the flour mixture and beat just until combined. Pour batter atop rhubarb. Bake at 350° for 50 to 60 minutes or until a toothpick inserted into the center comes out clean. Cool 5 minutes. Loosen the cake at the sides of the pan with a knife and invert it onto a serving plate.

Serve warm with whipped cream or vanilla ice cream. Can also be served at room temperature.

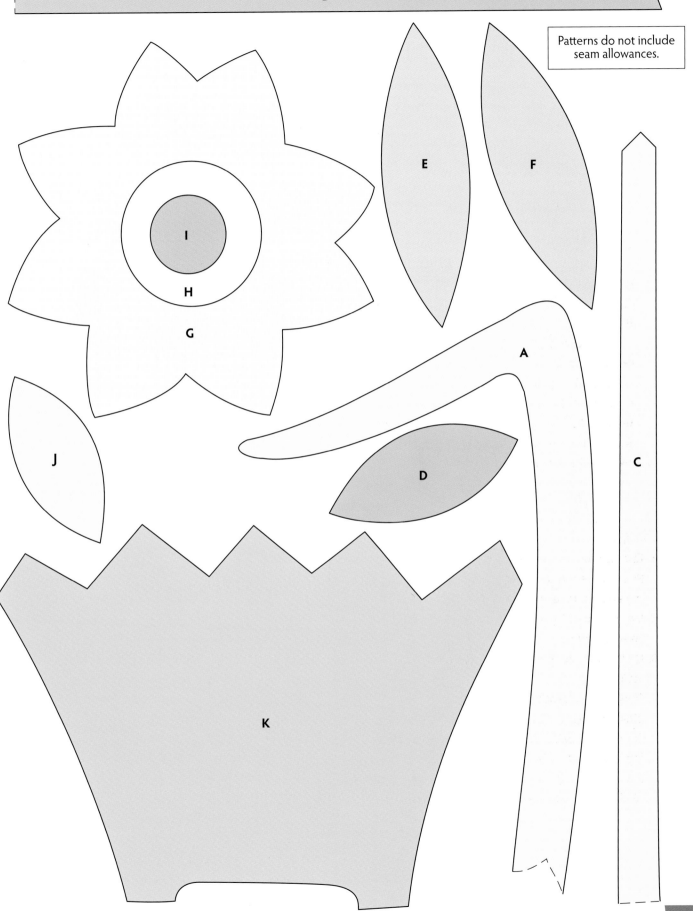

Patterns do not include seam allowances.

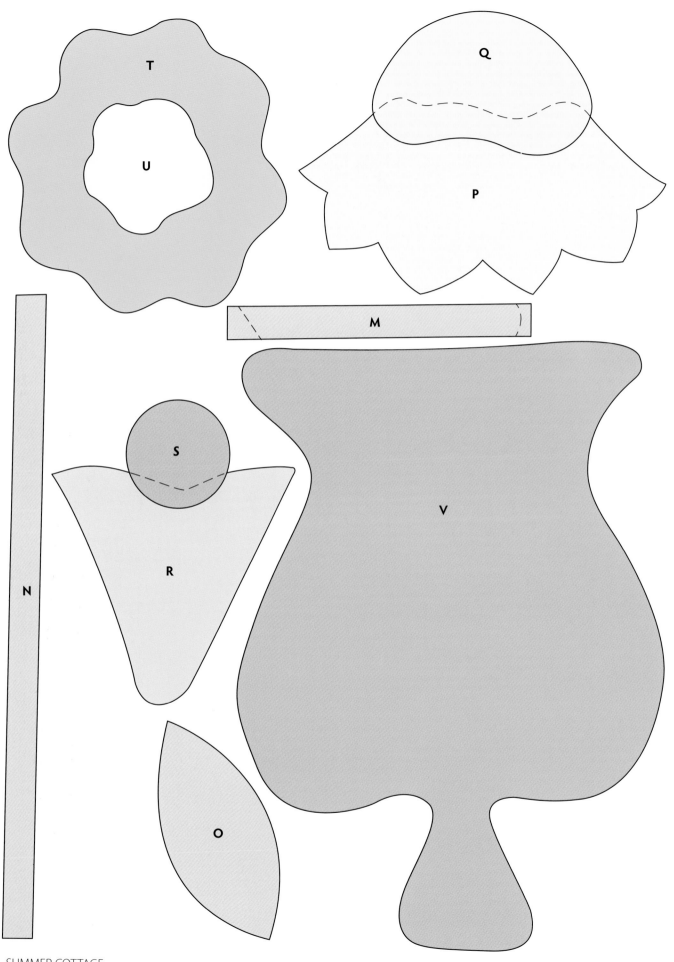

Patterns do not include
seam allowances.

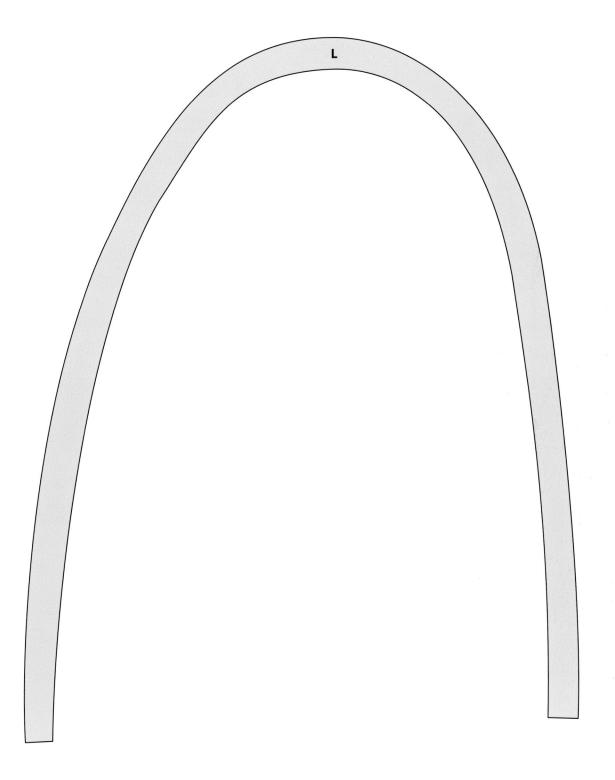

L

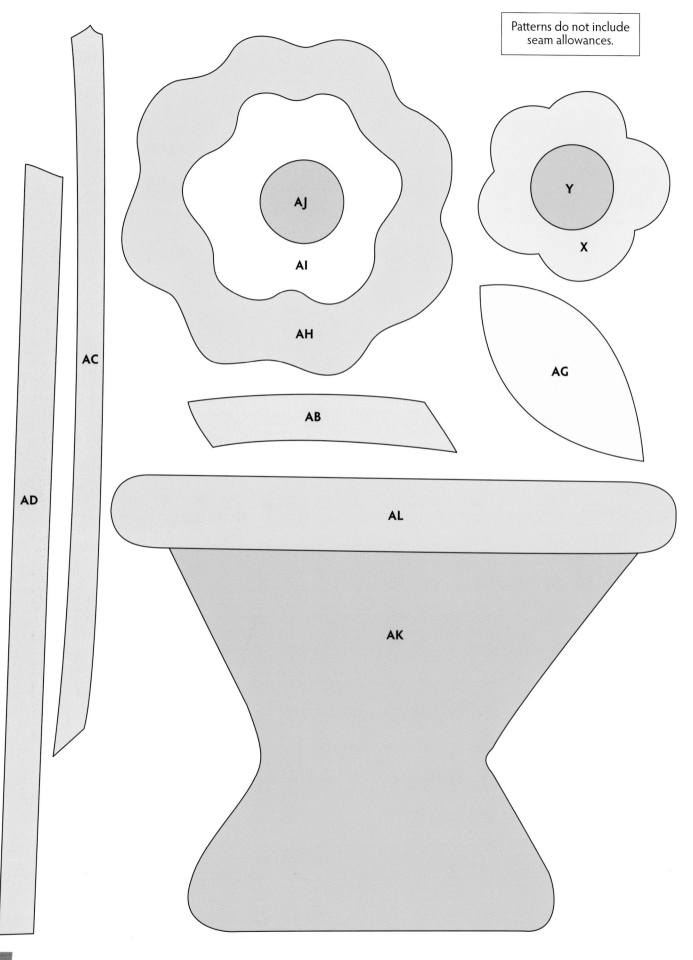

Patterns do not include
seam allowances.

AJ

AI

AH

AC

AD

AB

AG

Y

X

AL

AK

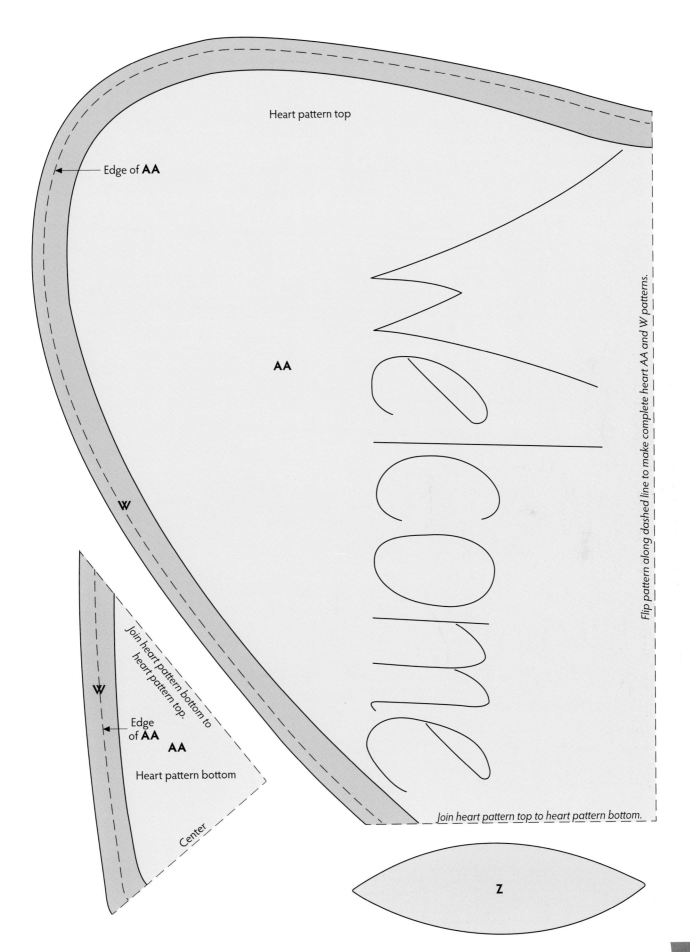

Heart pattern top

Edge of **AA**

AA

W

welcome

Flip pattern along dashed line to make complete heart AA and W patterns.

Join heart pattern bottom to heart pattern top.

W

Edge of **AA**

AA

Heart pattern bottom

Center

Join heart pattern top to heart pattern bottom.

Z

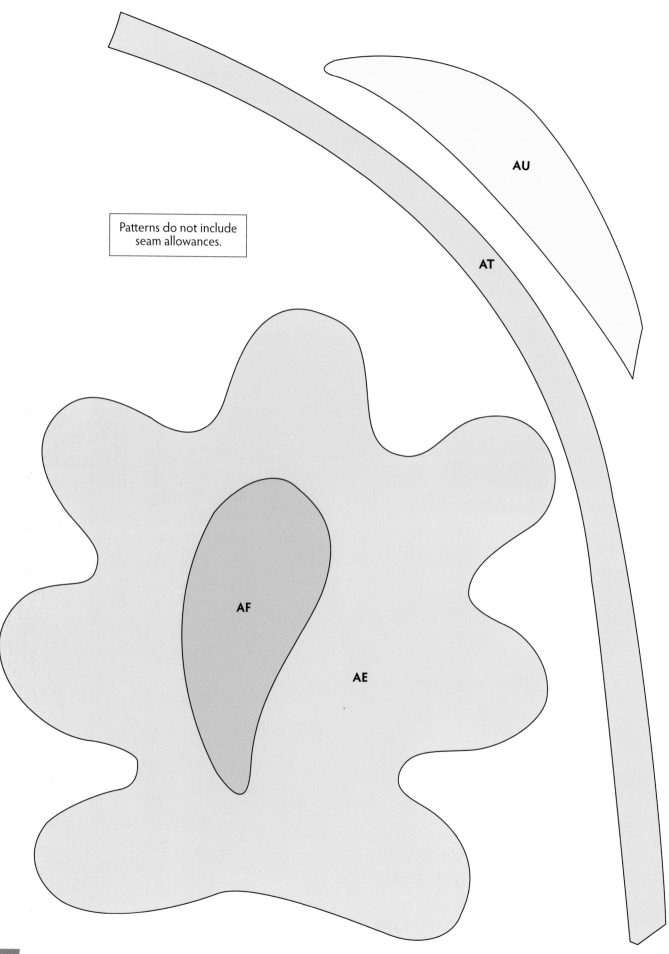

Patterns do not include
seam allowances.

AU

AT

AF

AE

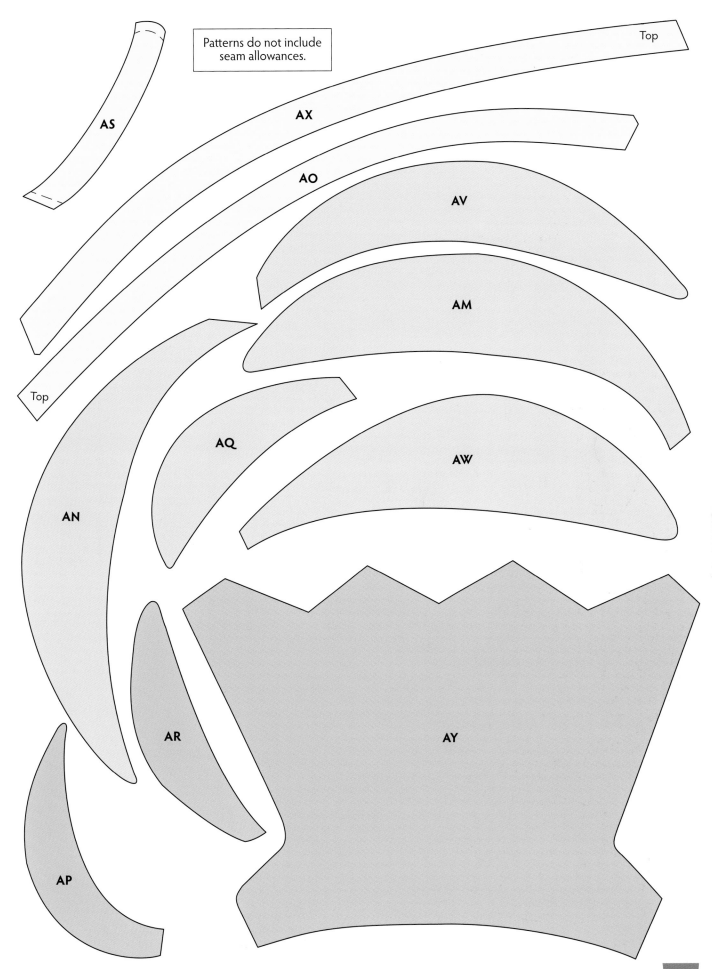

Patterns do not include
seam allowances.

AS

AX

Top

AO

AV

AM

AQ

AW

AN

Top

AR

AY

AP

Appliqué patterns do not include seam allowances.

BA

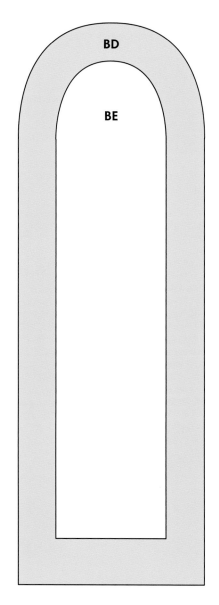

BD

BE

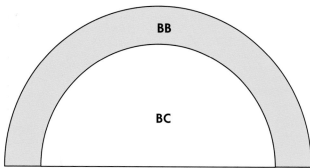

BB

BC

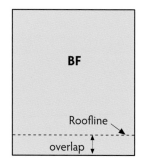

BF

Roofline

overlap

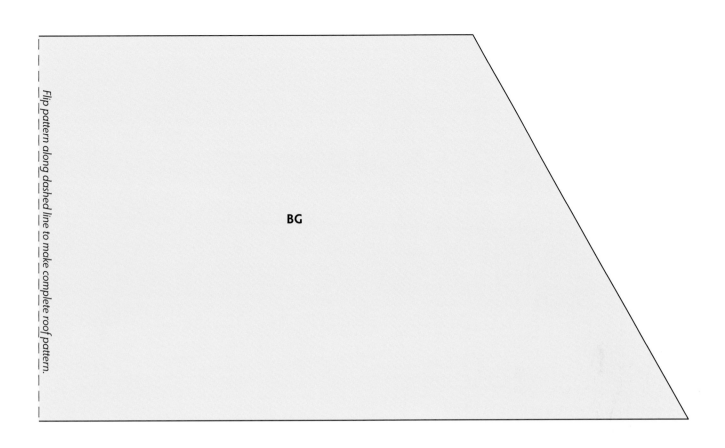

Flip pattern along dashed line to make complete roof pattern.

BG

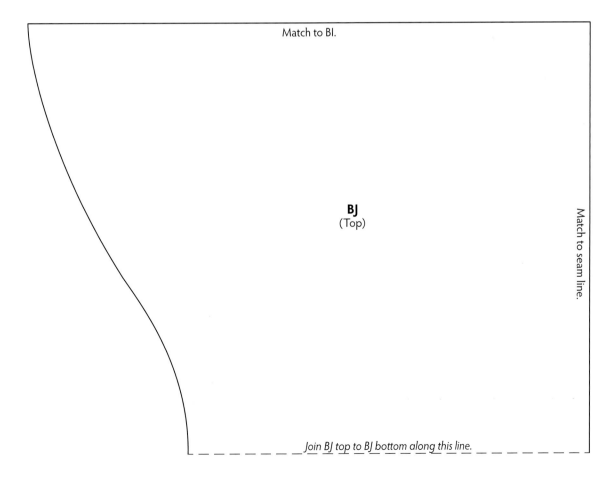

Match to BI.

Match to seam line.

BJ
(Top)

Join BJ top to BJ bottom along this line.

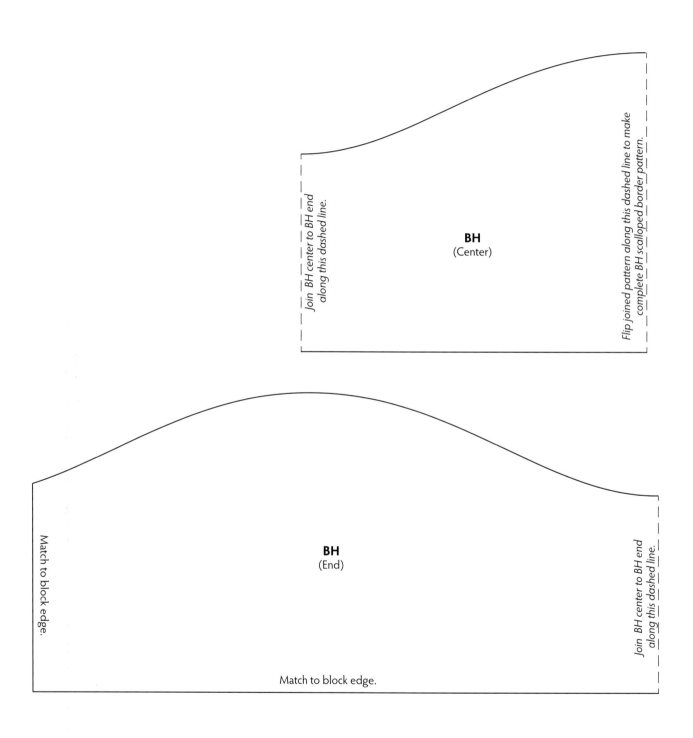

BH
(Center)

Join BH center to BH end along this dashed line.

Flip joined pattern along this dashed line to make complete BH scalloped border pattern.

BH
(End)

Match to block edge.

Match to block edge.

Join BH center to BH end along this dashed line.

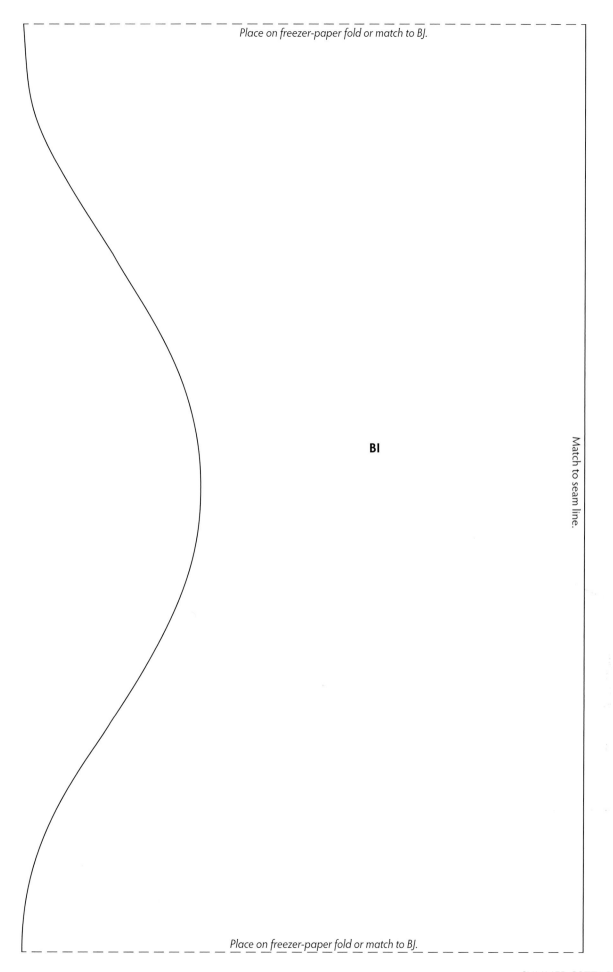

Place on freezer-paper fold or match to BJ.

BI

Match to seam line.

Place on freezer-paper fold or match to BJ.

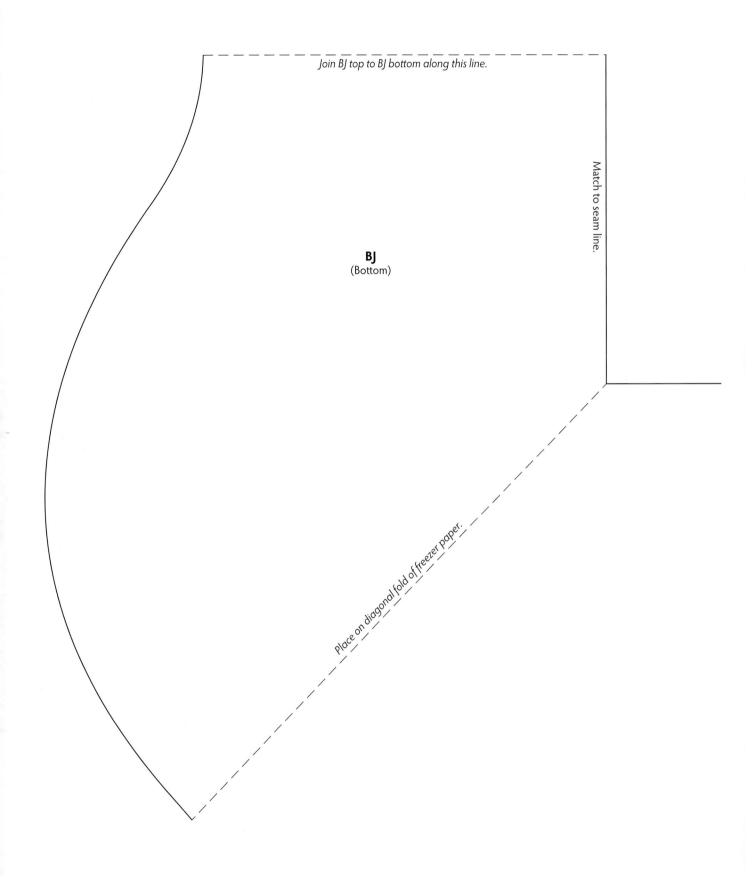

Join BJ top to BJ bottom along this line.

Match to seam line.

BJ
(Bottom)

Place on diagonal fold of freezer paper.

Rose Essential

Designed by Barbara Jones of QuiltSoup, pieced by Diane Erickson,
bound by Jan Child, and machine quilted by Catherine Timmons

Finished quilt: 54" x 66" • **Finished blocks:** 10" x 10"

This cheerful quilt is entirely pieced with no added appliqué. I named it after one of my favorite perfumes, since I could almost smell the rose fragrance as I was sewing these pretty floral fabrics together. I think this quilt would be a fabulous gift for a friend in need of a pick-me-up— I don't see how it could help but cheer someone up!

Materials

Yardage is based on 42"-wide fabric.

1⅞ yards of pink checked fabric for border

1 yard *total* of assorted blue prints for blocks

1 yard of cream solid for sashing

¾ yard *total* of assorted white prints for blocks

½ yard *total* of assorted pink prints for plain squares

½ yard *total* of assorted yellow prints for plain squares

¼ yard of green checked fabric for blocks and sashing

⅛ yard *each* of 3 green florals for sashing squares

⅛ yard *total* of assorted red prints for centers of blocks

½ yard of peach print for binding

3½ yards of fabric for backing

58" x 70" piece of batting

Cutting

Cutting for all patchwork pieces includes ¼" seam allowances.

From the pink checked fabric, cut:

2 *lengthwise* strips, 3½" x 60½"

2 *lengthwise* strips, 3½" x 54½"

From the assorted blue prints, cut:

40 *sets of 4* matching rectangles, 1⅞" x 3½" (160 total)

From the cream solid, cut:

12 strips, 2½" x 42"; crosscut into 31 rectangles, 2½" x 10½", and 18 rectangles, 2½" x 5½"

From the assorted white prints, cut:

40 squares, 4¼" x 4¼"; cut into quarters diagonally to yield 160 quarter-square triangles

2 squares, 5½" x 5½"

From the assorted pink prints, cut:

18 squares, 5½" x 5½"

From the assorted yellow prints, cut:

17 squares, 5½" x 5½"

From the green checked fabric, cut:

3 squares, 5½" x 5½"

4 squares, 2½" x 2½"

From the 3 green florals, cut a *total* of:

16 squares, 2½" x 2½"

From the assorted red prints, cut:

40 squares, 1⅞" x 1⅞"

Make the X Units

You'll need 40 X units for this quilt; 24 will be sewn into full blocks, 14 will be joined into half blocks, and 2 will be used as single corner blocks. The finished X units measure 5½" prior to joining them into the full or half blocks.

1. Sew matching white-print triangles to opposite long sides of a blue 1⅞" x 3½" rectangle as shown. Make sure the end of the rectangle is even with the right-angle edge of the triangles. The other end of the rectangle will extend beyond the points of the triangles and will be trimmed later. Repeat to make a matching unit. Press the seam allowances toward the blue rectangles.

Make 40 pairs
of matching units;
80 total.

2. Sew a red square between two matching blue rectangles; press the seam allowances toward the rectangles.

3. Sew the triangle units from step 1 to opposite sides of the rectangle unit from step 2, matching the seam intersections. Press the seam allowances toward the triangle units.

4. Using a square ruler and a rotary cutter, trim the corners of the blocks to square them up. The finished X unit should measure 5½" x 5½". Repeat all steps to make a total of 40 X units.

Make 40.

Assemble the Blocks

1. Using the X units and the 5½" squares, join two X units and two squares in a four-patch arrangement as shown. Press the seam allowances toward the plain squares. Repeat to make 12 of these full blocks.

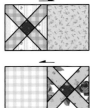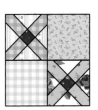

Full block.
Make 12.

2. Join one X unit and one 5½" square to make a half block. Repeat to make 14 half blocks. Press the seam allowances toward the plain squares. You'll have two X units and two 5½" squares left over to use in the quilt corners.

Half block.
Make 14.

Assemble the Quilt Top

1. Sew a green 2½" square to one end of a cream 2½" x 5½" sashing strip. Make 10.

Make 10.

2. Join three cream 2½" x 10½" sashing strips and two green squares as shown. Make five. Sew a short sashing unit from step 1 to each end of each strip to complete the sashing rows.

Make 5.

3. Lay out the blocks, half blocks, sashing rows, and sashing strips following the quilt layout diagram below. Rearrange until you're pleased with the color placement. Sew the pieces together in rows; press the seam allowances toward the sashing strips. Note that the single X units are placed in the top-left corner (row 1) and bottom-right corner (row 6).

4. Sew a 3½" x 60½" border strip to each side of the quilt top. Add the 3½" x 54½" strips to the top and bottom. Press the seam allowances toward the border strips.

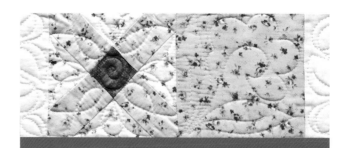

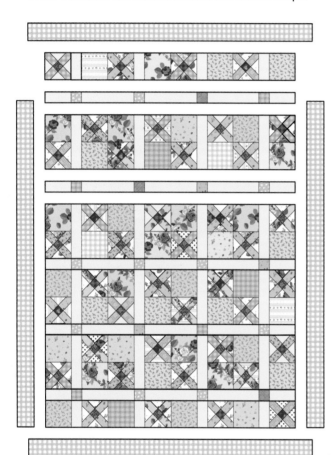

Finish the Quilt

1. Prepare the backing fabric so that it's approximately 4" larger than the quilt top in both directions. Layer the quilt top, batting, and backing and baste the layers together.

2. Quilt as desired.

3. Trim the backing and batting to match the quilt top, squaring the corners.

4. From the binding fabric, cut enough 2¼"-wide bias strips to equal 280".

5. Bind the edges as detailed in "Binding" (page 94).

Amaretto Scones

For some reason, this quilt makes me think of tea and scones! Here's one of my favorite scone recipes.

INGREDIENTS

½ cup raisins
2 cups all-purpose flour
2 teaspoons baking powder
⅓ cup cold unsalted butter, cut into pieces
¼ cup milk
½ cup chopped walnuts or pecans
1 Tablespoon Amaretto, or to taste
⅓ cup granulated sugar
½ teaspoon baking soda
1 egg, beaten
¼ cup, plus 2 tablespoons, heavy cream
Confectioner's sugar for dusting

Before starting scones, place raisins in a bowl and cover with Amaretto. Cover with plastic wrap and refrigerate for at least 1 hour or until raisins have plumped. Combine dry ingredients in a bowl. Cut in butter with a pastry cutter until mixture resembles crumbs.

In another bowl, mix together the egg, milk, cream, and Amaretto (reserving the raisins). Pour into dry ingredients and mix until just combined. Add the raisins and nuts. Mix until a dough comes together. Turn dough onto a lightly floured surface and knead lightly. With a round cutter (2" or 3"), cut dough. Space scones at least 1" to 2" apart on an ungreased cookie sheet. Brush the top of each scone with the remaining cream. Bake the scones at 350° for 12 to 14 minutes, or until scones are light brown in color. Let scones cool, and then dust with confectioner's sugar.

Ellery's Smoothie

Pieced and appliquéd by Barbara Jones; quilted by Sue McCarty

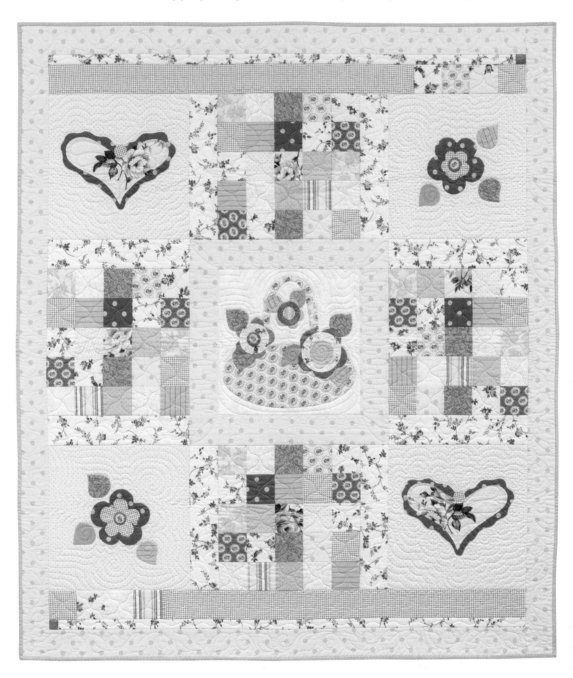

Finished quilt: 57" x 65" • **Finished blocks:** 15" x 15"

One of the first patterns QuiltSoup produced was called "Strawberry Smoothie." We had such fun making it that we remade it when we produced our first line of fabric, called Ellery after my granddaughter. The appliqué in this pattern is presented with the easiest blocks first. The alternate pieced blocks are scrappy and simple.

Materials

Yardage is based on 42"-wide fabric.

2 yards of yellow-and-pink print for borders and pieced blocks

1 yard of cream small floral for sashing, pieced blocks, appliqué, and border

1 yard of yellow pindot for appliqué backgrounds and pieced blocks

⅝ yard of cream-and-pink floral for Basket block background, pieced blocks, and appliqué

½ yard of red polka-dot fabric for appliqué and pieced blocks

⅓ yard of red gingham for appliqué, pieced blocks, and inner borders

⅓ yard of pink large floral for appliqué

⅓ yard of yellow cameo print for basket appliqué

¼ yard of red tone-on-tone fabric for appliqué

⅛ yard *each* of 4 assorted green fabrics for appliqué and pieced blocks

⅛ yard *each* of 6 assorted cream, pink, yellow, and red fabrics for appliqué and pieced blocks

⅔ yard of salmon pindot for binding

3½ yards of fabric for backing

61" x 66" piece of batting

Template plastic

Basic appliqué tool kit (see page 6)

Assorted Fabrics

Among the assorted fabrics I used are a red cameo print, the salmon pindot (also used for the binding), a small pink floral, and coordinating striped fabrics. Cut all the other quilt pieces, including the backing and binding, first; then use the leftover fabrics for the pieced blocks and appliqué patches.

Cutting

Appliqué patterns are on pages 88–93. Cutting for all patchwork pieces includes ¼" seam allowances.

From the yellow-and-pink print, cut:

2 *lengthwise* strips, 3½" x 65½"

2 *lengthwise* strips, 3½" x 51½"

2 rectangles, 3½" x 15½"

2 rectangles, 3½" x 21½"

1 using pattern K

From the cream small floral, cut:

8 rectangles, 3½" x 15½"

3 strips, 1½" x 42"

1 using pattern J

From the yellow pindot, cut:

2 strips, 16½" x 42"; crosscut into 4 squares, 16½" x 16½"

From the cream-and-pink floral, cut:

1 strip, 16½" x 42"; crosscut into 1 square, 16½" x 16½"

From the red polka-dot fabric, cut:

2 using pattern A

2 using pattern D

1 using pattern M

From the red gingham, cut:

2 strips, 3½" x 39½"

2 using pattern C

2 using pattern E

From the pink large floral, cut:

2 using pattern B

From the yellow cameo print, cut:

1 using pattern G

1 using pattern H

From the red tone-on-tone, cut:

2 squares, 1½" x 1½"

1 using pattern I

1 using pattern X

From the assorted greens, cut:

3 *each* using patterns R, S, and T (9 total)

1 *each* using patterns P, Q, U, and V

1 rectangle from *each* fabric, 3½" x 18" (4 total)

From the assorted prints and leftover fabrics, cut:

21 strips, 3½" x 18"

8 squares, 3½" x 3½"

2 using pattern F

1 *each* using patterns L, N, O, and Y

1 using pattern W

Fancy Flowers

Experiment with fussy cutting appliqué circles for the flower centers, as I did with the medium and extra-large flowers.

Make the Pieced Blocks

1. Sew five assorted 3½" x 18" strips together to make one strip set. Press all the seam allowances in the same direction. Make five sets.

2. From each strip set, crosscut four 3½" x 15½" rectangles as shown.

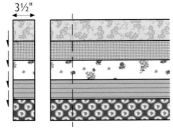

3½"

Make 5 assorted strip sets.
Cut 4 segments from each.

3. Arrange the pieced rectangles in random groups of five. Rotate alternate rectangles so the seam allowances lie in opposite directions.

4. Sew each group together into a 25 Patch block. Make four.

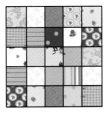

25 Patch block.
Make 4.

Make the Appliqué Blocks

1. **Heart blocks:** Using the photo and illustration as a guide, layer a red heart (A), a pink heart (B), and a gingham circle (C) at the center of a yellow pindot square. Glue baste and appliqué the shapes in order. Make two.

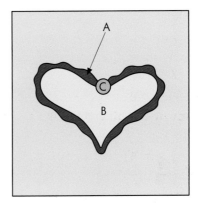

Heart block.
Make 2.

2. **Flower blocks:** Stack a red flower (D), a gingham flower (E), and a flower center (F) on a yellow pindot square. Arrange leaves R, S, and T around the flower as shown. Glue baste and appliqué each shape. Make two.

Flower block.
Make 2.

Easy Vs

All the sharp "cleavage" points on the medium and large flowers are meant to be covered by the next patch. You won't have to work any sharp V points!

3. Basket block: Assemble the large flower from the I, J, K, and L patches using the unit appliqué method (page 13) and cutting away the excess fabric behind each new layer as it's added. Appliqué circle J on top of flower I, turning the circle seam allowances to the wrong side between the flower petals. Cut away the excess fabric behind J, leaving a ¼" seam allowance inside the marked stitching line. Stitch L on top of K in the same way. Layer the K/L unit on top of the J/I unit and appliqué K to J; trim the excess fabric from behind.

Assemble the small and medium flowers using the unit appliqué method. Arrange the handle, basket, flowers, and leaves on the cream-and-pink floral background square as shown. Glue baste and stitch the appliqués to the background fabric.

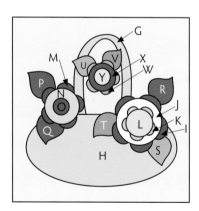

Basket block.
Make 1.

4. Press and trim all five appliqué blocks to 15½" x 15½".

Assemble the Sashing and Border

1. Sew a cream floral 3½" x 15½" strip to each end of a yellow-and-pink 3½" x 21½" strip. Press toward the cream rectangles. Make two. These are the horizontal sashing units.

Make 2.

2. Sew the cream floral 1½" strips together end to end, making one continuous length. Cut the assembled unit into two 50½" strips. Sew a red tone-on-tone 1½" square to one end of each strip. Press the seam allowances toward the red squares. Make two.

3. Sew four assorted 3½" squares together in any order. Press all the seam allowances in one direction. Make two. Sew each unit to one end of a red gingham 39½" strip. Make two.

Fool the Eye

To add continuity to the gingham border strips, I used the same red gingham as the final square in each group of four, making the other three squares appear to float on a gingham strip.

4. Sew a strip from step 2 to the bottom of a yellow-and-pink 51½" strip as shown. Press the seam allowances toward the yellow-and-pink. Sew a pieced gingham strip to the bottom of the cream floral strip. Press the seam allowances toward the cream floral strip. Make two. These are the top and bottom border units.

Top and bottom border unit.
Make 2.

Turn Around

The top and bottom border units are identical, with one rotated 180° in the finished quilt.

Assemble the Quilt Top

1. Lay out the blocks, sashing, and borders as shown. Sew 15½" sashing strips between the blocks in each row and press the seam allowances as directed in the illustrations.
2. Sew border units to the top of row 1 and the bottom of row 3.

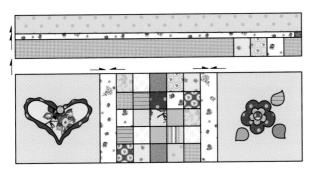

Row 1 and top border unit

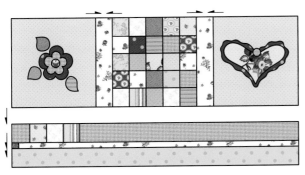

Row 3 and bottom border unit

3. Attach horizontal sashing units to the top and bottom of row 2 and press the seam allowances toward the sashing. Sew the three rows together to complete the quilt center.

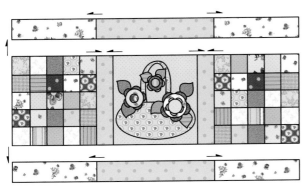

Row 2 and horizontal sashing

4. Sew the yellow-and-pink 65½" strips to the sides of the quilt. Press the seam allowances toward the borders.

Finish the Quilt

1. Cut the backing into two 61" lengths. Remove the selvages and sew the two sections together along one long edge. Layer the quilt top, batting, and backing and baste the layers together.
2. Quilt as desired.
3. Trim the backing and batting to match the quilt top, squaring the corners.
4. From the binding fabric, cut enough 2¼"-wide bias strips to equal 280". Bind the edges as detailed in "Binding" (page 94).
5. Put your feet up, enjoy a smoothie, and pat yourself on the back!

Strawberry Smoothie

INGREDIENTS

2 cups fresh or frozen strawberries

½ cup milk

⅔ cup vanilla yogurt

½ cup orange juice

½ cup ice cubes

Mix all ingredients in a blender until smooth. Garnish with a halved berry or orange slice. Chill in the freezer for 30 minutes. Serves 4.

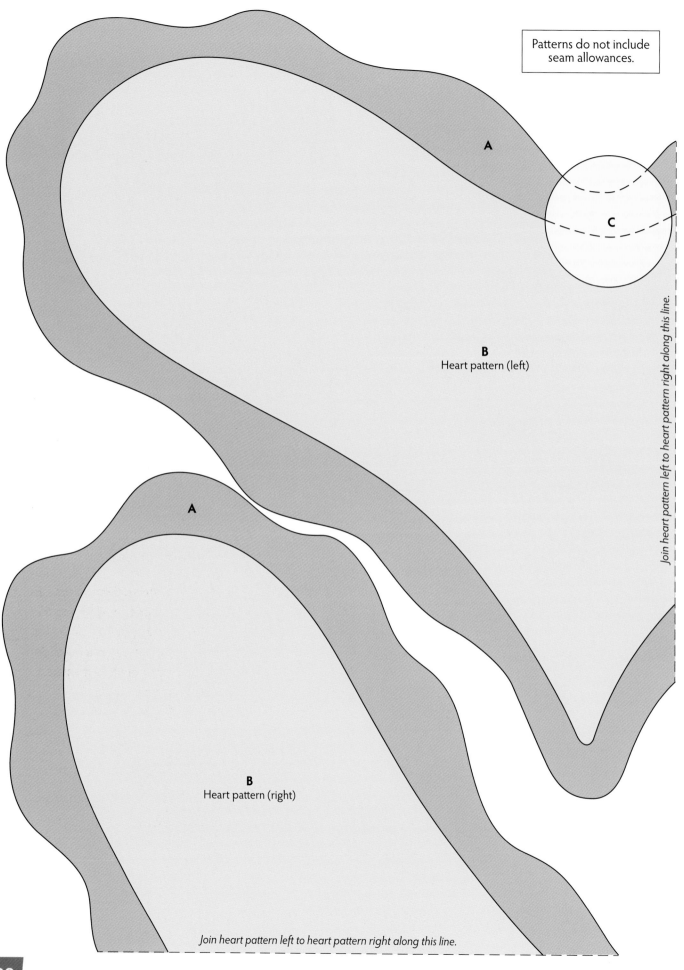

Patterns do not include seam allowances.

A

C

B
Heart pattern (left)

Join heart pattern left to heart pattern right along this line.

A

B
Heart pattern (right)

Join heart pattern left to heart pattern right along this line.

The author cut one E shape smaller than the other; see the photo on page 83. You may do this, or make them both the same.

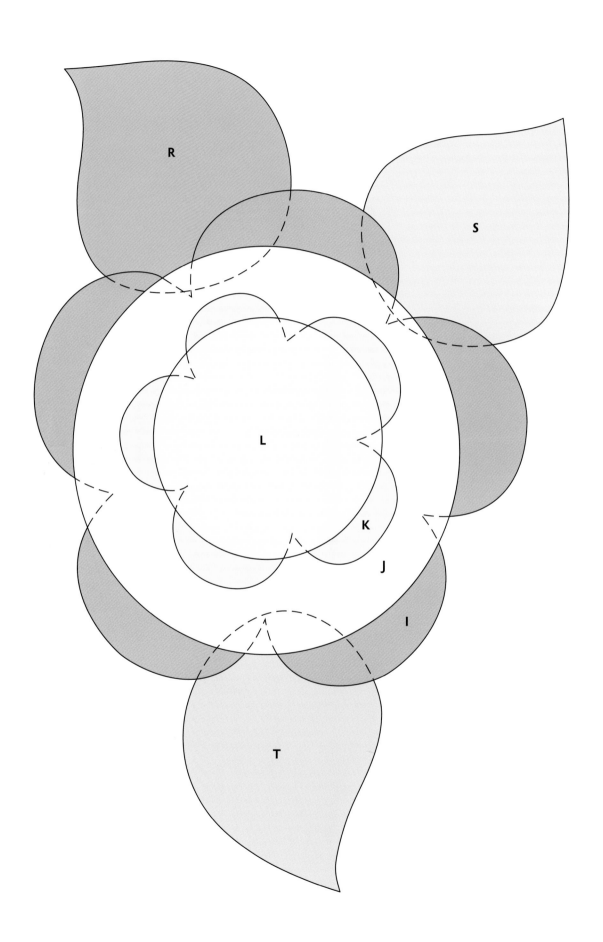

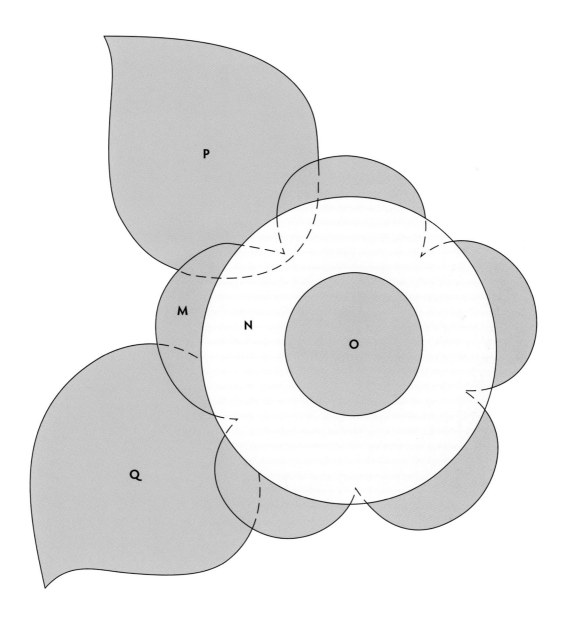

Patterns do not include seam allowances.

P

M

N

O

Q

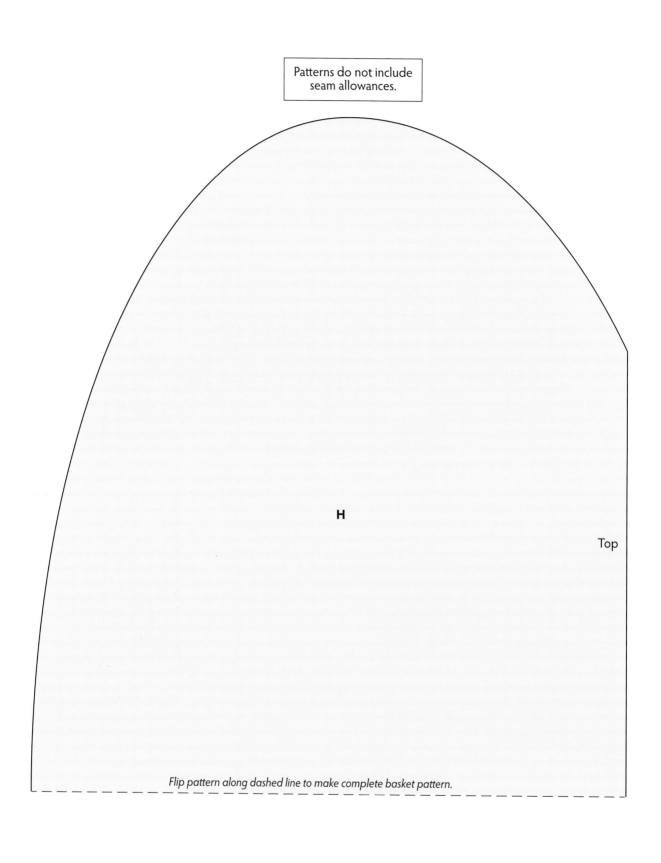

Patterns do not include seam allowances.

H

Top

Flip pattern along dashed line to make complete basket pattern.

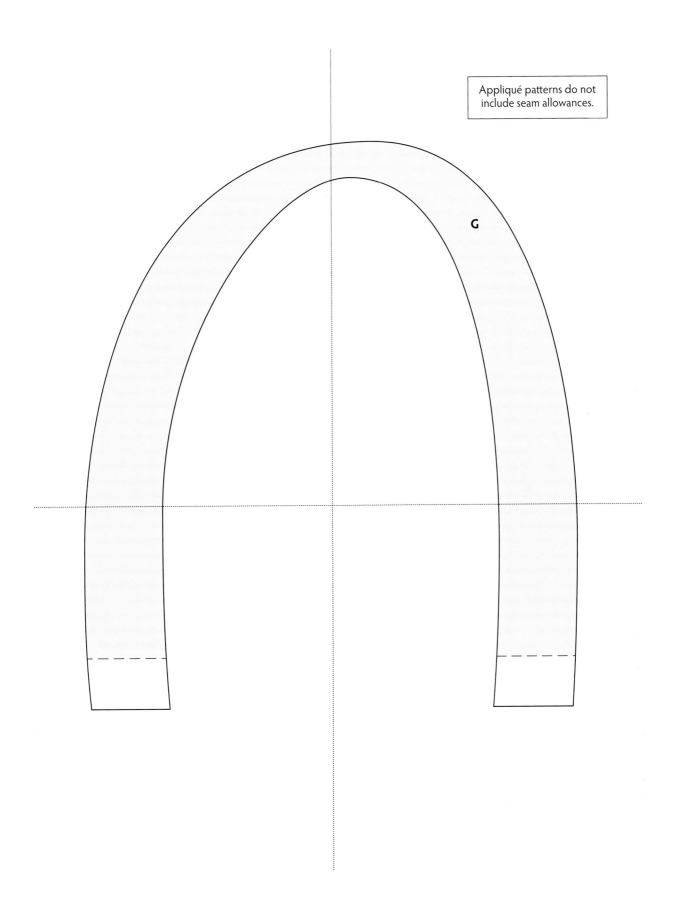

Appliqué patterns do not
include seam allowances.

G

Basic Quiltmaking Instructions

You'll find some necessary information on the non-appliqué parts of the quiltmaking process here. If you require more help, visit ShopMartingale.com/HowToQuilt for free downloadable information.

The Quilt Sandwich

The back of a quilt can be anything from a simple backing with no seams to a potpourri of random patchwork and appliqué that's a quilt in its own right; the choice is completely yours. If you plan to hand quilt, remember that fewer thicknesses (fabric layers and seam allowances) are easier to quilt through; a simple backing may be the best choice. If you or a professional machine quilter will be quilting by machine, you have more freedom to design a complex quilt backing.

Frugal Backing

I often use any test blocks I've made as well as fabric scraps on the back of the quilt. It's frugal and fun!

Make a quilt backing that's 4" larger in both width and length than the quilt top. Press the backing well, and then fold it in half horizontally and vertically to find the center. Cut the batting 4" wider and longer than the quilt top as well and fold it as for the backing. Press the finished quilt top for the final time and fold it to mark the center lines.

Lay the quilt backing fabric right side down on a large table or a clean floor. Place the batting over the backing, matching the edges. Lay the quilt top right side up, matching the centerlines on all three layers.

Pin baste in a 2" to 3" grid using safety pins, beginning with the vertical and horizontal centerlines. Baste one quarter of the quilt at a time.

Go Pro

As a treat to yourself from time to time (or all the time), consider hiring a professional quilter to layer, baste, and quilt. A good quilter is worth her weight in gold.

Binding

I use double-fold bias bindings for all of my quilts; I think they lie and wear better. A bias binding is absolutely necessary for curves, whether rounded corners or scalloped edges.

Begin by identifying the fabric's true bias, which lies at a 45° angle from the selvage.

Cut the required number of bias strips, 2¼" wide, along the true bias.

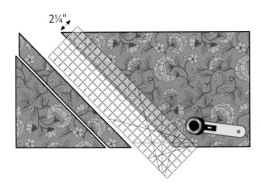

When all the strips are cut, trim both ends of each strip at the same angle. Sew the strips end to end into one continuous length. Press the seam allowances open.

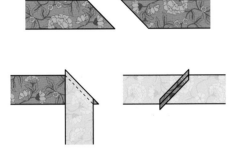

Fold the long strip in half lengthwise, wrong sides together, and press the fold. Lay the binding on the quilt's right side, matching the raw edges, with the end of the binding near the center of one quilt edge. Begin sewing about 6" from the leading end of the binding. Sew along the side of the quilt to a point ¼" from the corner. Backstitch and cut the thread. Fold the binding up at a 90° angle.

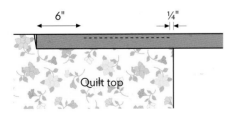

Quilt top

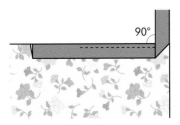

90°

Fold the binding back on itself along the quilt edge, aligning it with the next side of the quilt. Reposition the quilt under the needle for sewing the next side and begin sewing again at the corner. Repeat around the quilt to a point about 12" before the first binding stitches.

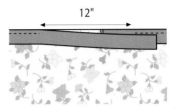

12"

Smooth both ends of the binding into place on the quilt. Mark and trim the ends, leaving a 2¼" overlap. Unfold the binding ends. Lay one end on the other, right sides together, at right angles. Sew across the square formed where the binding ends overlap. Trim away the excess fabric, leaving a ¼" seam allowance. Press the seam open. Refold the binding and sew it to the remainder of the quilt edge.

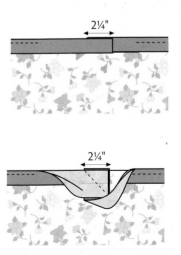

2¼"

2¼"

Bring the binding's folded edge over the raw edge of the quilt to the back. Blind stitch the fold to the quilt back, just covering the seam.

About the Author

Barbara Jones has been a quiltmaker for the past 25 years or so. She loves everything about quilting except binding, which she has finally learned to hire out! Her passion is appliqué and her company, QuiltSoup, specializes in appliqué patterns for beginning to intermediate stitchers. Her design style is whimsical and contemporary.

Barbara also designs fabric for Henry Glass & Co. Fabrics—she recently put the finishing touches on her seventh (or so) collection for them. She draws the designs for each collection and sometimes throws in a vintage print for good measure. She prefers to give a bit of an eclectic look to a collection. She is also the author of several quilting books and booklets.

She has one son and daughter-in-law and five beautiful grandchildren who often serve as inspiration for her designs. She lived in the Salt Lake City area for about 40 years, but recently moved to a tiny town in Idaho, which is her ancestral homeland.

Visit Barbara online at www.QuiltSoup.com.

What's your creative passion?
Find it at ShopMartingale.com

books • eBooks • ePatterns • daily blog • free projects
videos • tutorials • inspiration • giveaways